The Rainbow
A Search for New Life

TWAYNE'S MASTERWORK STUDIES
Robert Lecker, General Editor

The Rainbow
A Search for New Life

Duane Edwards

Twayne Publishers • Boston
A Division of G.K. Hall & Co.

The Rainbow: A Search for New Life
Duane Edwards

Twayne's Masterwork Studies No. 51
Copyright 1990 by G.K. Hall & Co.
All rights reserved.
Published by Twayne Publishers
A division of G.K. Hall & Co.
70 Lincoln Street, Boston, Massachusetts 02111

Copyediting supervised by Barbara Sutton.
Book production by Gabrielle B. McDonald.
Typeset in 10/14 Sabon with ITC Zapf Chancery display type
by Compositors Corporation of Cedar Rapids, Iowa.

Printed on permanent/durable acid-free paper
and bound in the United States of America.

Library of Congress Cataloging-in-Publication Data

Edwards, Duane.
    The rainbow : a search for new life / Duane Edwards.
      p. cm. — (Twayne's masterwork studies ; no. 51)
    Includes bibliographical references.
    1. Lawrence, D. H. (David Herbert), 1885–1930. Rainbow. I. Title.
II. Series
PR6023.A93R3337   1990
823'.912—dc20   *89-26819*
                                                   CIP

0-8057-9401-8 (alk. paper). 10 9 8 7 6 5 4 3 2 1
0-8057-8129-3 (pbk. alk. paper). 10 9 8 7 6 5 4 3 2 1
First published 1990

Contents

A Reading

v

Note on the References and Acknowledgments

All page references to *The Rainbow* (first published by Methuen in 1915) are to the 1987 Viking Penguin edition (New York) and appear in parentheses in the text.

I would like to thank Viking Penguin Inc. for granting me permission to quote from *The Rainbow*. Copyright 1915 by David Herbert Lawrence. Copyright 1943 by Frieda Lawrence. All rights reserved.

I would like to thank those people at Fairleigh Dickinson University, Rutherford, New Jersey, who supported me as I wrote this work: the library staff of Messler Library, members of the College Research Advisory Committee, and Dr. Mordechai Rozanski, dean of the College of Liberal Arts.

Finally, I would like to thank Keith Cushman, professor of English at the University of North Carolina at Greensboro and president of the D. H. Lawrence Society of North America, who loaned me the photograph that is the frontispiece of this book.

D. H. Lawrence
Photo courtesy of Keith Cushman

Chronology:
D. H. Lawrence's
Life and Works

1885   David Herbert Lawrence born 11 September to Arthur and Lydia Lawrence at Eastwood, Nottinghamshire, a mining village near Sherwood Forest.

1898   Enrolls in Nottingham High School on 14 September after winning a scholarship. Rev. Robert Reid becomes the local Congregational minister and is soon a friend of Mrs. Lawrence. (In 1907 Lawrence writes letters about religion to Rev. Reid.)

1901   Death of Lawrence's oldest brother, William Ernest, the model for William in *Sons and Lovers*. Lawrence meets Jessie Chambers, his first sweetheart and the model for Miriam in *Sons and Lovers*, at the Haggs.

1902   Begins work as an uncertified teacher at Eastwood. Ill for a month with pneumonia.

1904   Finishes first in all of England and Wales in the King's Scholarship examination.

1906   Enters University College, Nottingham, for a teacher training course.

1908   Receives teacher's certificate in June and begins a short but successful teaching career at Davidson Road School where he has large classes, paints scenery for class plays, and receives favorable reviews of his teaching.

1909   Jessie Chambers sends Lawrence's poems to Ford Madox Ford, who publishes them in the *English Review*.

1910   Heinemann accepts *The White Peacock*. More poems published in the *English Review*. Breaks off engagement with Jessie Chambers. Mrs. Lawrence receives an advance copy of *The White Peacock* before she dies of cancer on 9 December.

1911   Suffers from pneumonia and calls 1911 his "sick year." Continues to work on *Sons and Lovers*. *The White Peacock* published in January. "Odour of Chrysanthemums" appears in the *English Review.*

1912   Breaks engagement with Louie Burrows. Meets Frieda who is married to Ernest Weekley, a professor of French. Elopes with Frieda and crosses the Channel on 3 May. *The Trespasser* is published. Revises *Sons and Lovers* and completes it in November under Frieda's influence. In December, vows always to be "a priest of love."

1913   *Sons and Lovers* published on 29 May. Works on "The Sisters," which later becomes *The Rainbow* and *Women in Love*. Comments in letters about Frieda's positive influence on him. Returns to England after a trip to Germany and Italy with Frieda.

1914   Marries Frieda on 13 July after insisting on a formal ceremony. Comments in letters on his happiness with Frieda. *The Prussian Officer* published. England enters war against Germany while Lawrence and friends are on a walking tour of the Lake District. Begins and finishes his *Study of Thomas Hardy.* On 5 June writes his famous letter to Edward Garnett about the new kind of character who appears in *The Rainbow.*

1915   *The Rainbow* is published. Negative reviews appear almost at once. In November the novel is suppressed. In letters expresses his horror and sorrow over the war. Moves with Frieda to Cornwall.

1916   Finishes *Women in Love*. Expresses his fondness for Cornwall. Announces the end of his "bloody fight" with Frieda as it is recorded in the poems called *Look! We Have Come Through!* Takes medical examination for the army and is pronounced completely exempt. Says he is in a "black fury" over the war.

1917   Publishes *Look! We Have Come Through!* Is expelled from Cornwall on suspicion of spying for and aiding the Germans.

1918   Writes *The Fox*. Publishes *New Poems*. Is examined again by the army.

1919   Nearly dies of influenza. Poverty and neglect are major problems for Lawrence. He and Frieda take separate vacations on the Continent but meet in Capri.

1920   Completes *The Lost Girl*. Works on *Mr. Noon*, which does not appear in print in complete form until 1984. Meets Maurice Magnus, the lovable parasite who commits suicide after Lawrence decides to discontinue giving him money. *Women in Love* published in a limited edition. Admits he has writer's block halfway through *Aaron's Rod*. Refers to himself as a "charity-boy of literature."

1921 Visits Sardinia and writes *Sea and Sardinia*. Receives the James Tait Black prize of one hundred pounds for *The Lost Girl* (his first and last award). *Psychoanalysis and the Unconscious* published. Writes *Fantasia of the Unconscious* and finishes *Aaron's Rod*. Travels extensively in Europe. In letters expresses his disgust with the world of people and his love of natural beauty.

1922 *Aaron's Rod* and *Fantasia of the Unconscious* published. Travels to Ceylon where he becomes very ill. Goes to Australia and meets Molly Skinner, the woman who composed the first version of *The Boy in the Bush*. Writes nearly all of *Kangaroo* in six weeks. Goes to America where he visits San Francisco before meeting Mabel Luhan in Taos, New Mexico.

1923 *Kangaroo* published. Travels in Mexico with Frieda. Begins writing *The Plumed Serpent*, originally called "Quetzalcoatl." Arrives in New York City in July. Rewrites *The Boy in the Bush*.

1924 Spends time in England with Frieda, who has sailed from America without him after a quarrel. Behaves badly during the infamous "Last Supper" at the Café Royal in London. Returns to Taos by 22 March. Completes *St. Mawr*, "The Princess," and the controversial "The Woman Who Rode Away" during the summer. Returns to Mexico to continue work on *The Plumed Serpent*.

1925 Finishes *The Plumed Serpent* and immediately becomes ill. Dictates portions of "The Flying Fish" to Frieda because he is ill and weak. *St. Mawr* published. Visits England and finds the Midlands unpleasant. Writes a number of short stories including "Sun," "Smile," and "Glad Ghosts."

1926 *The Plumed Serpent* published. Begins writing *Lady Chatterley's Lover* in Italy. Visits the Haggs. On 3 December writes a nostalgic letter about Eastwood and the house in which he grew up.

1927 Comments in letters on the importance of the "societal impulse." Is seriously ill with influenza in February and March. Visits Etruscan tombs and begins *Etruscan Places*. Paints and continues to work on the second draft of *Lady Chatterley's Lover*.

1928 *Lady Chatterley's Lover* published in Italy. In December, announces a profit from the novel of over one thousand pounds. Writes "Autobiographical Sketch." On 10 November writes his famous letter about the "censor-morons." Writes a nostalgic letter about the Haggs on 14 November.

1929   Writes his last book, the posthumously published *Apocalypse.* Thousands of people see the exhibition of Lawrence's paintings in London. Police raid the gallery and take away thirteen paintings on 5 July. Writes two volumes of poems, *Nettles* and *Last Poems,* which includes "The Ship of Death," a poem about preparing for death. Is very ill but comments in a letter about the beauty of the countryside.

1930   *Nettles* published. Enters the Ad Astra sanitorium in Vence, France, on 6 February. Dies in Vence on 2 March at the age of forty-four.

1935   Ashes taken to New Mexico.

Chapter 1

Historical Context

On 16 May 1914 D. H. Lawrence announced that *The Rainbow* was finished. Promising to mail the manuscript to Edward Garnett on the following Monday, he added: "I am rather proud of it now."[1] Because he needed the three hundred pounds he expected for the English rights alone, he was also relieved. He was rather carefree when he began a walking tour of the Lake District with friends on the last day of July.

On 5 August, in the midst of his walking tour, he learned that Great Britain had declared war on Germany the previous day. Severely understating his reaction, he described himself as "very miserable about the war."[2] When he learned a few days later that his publisher had rejected his novel, he was even more miserable. After all, he had worked very hard on *The Rainbow,* having begun it "for about the seventh time"[3] by 9 February 1914. After so much hard work, he was convinced that he had produced "one of the important novels in the language."[4] Now, suddenly, he had to worry about where he would get the money he needed to support himself and Frieda, his wife.

Methuen's rejection of the novel on grounds of indecency was a great blow to Lawrence, but the war was a much greater blow. Reacting to its violence and senselessness, he felt much worse than the word "miserable" suggests. In a letter to Lady Cynthia Asquith he acknowledged his real reaction; he was devastated: "The War finished me: it was the spear through the side of all sorrows and hopes. I had been walking in Westmoreland, rather happy, with water-lilies twisted round my hat . . . and girls who had come out on a spree and who were having tea in the upper room of an inn shrieked with laughter. . . . Then we came down to Barrow in Furness, and saw that war was declared. And we all went mad." Commenting more specifically on his own condition, he went on to say, "All the while, I swear, my soul lay in the tomb."[5]

With his soul in the tomb, Lawrence had to make a choice. He could send the manuscript to another publisher, or he could revise it. He chose to revise. Given the state of the world and Lawrence's own emotional state, his decision is remarkable. Even more remarkable is the revision itself. As Lawrence told a friend, "I don't think the war altered it, from its pre-war statement." His claim that he "only clarified a little, in revision,"[6] however, is suspect, for, as Charles Ross observes in his very valuable and interesting study of the history of the novel's revisions, "Prima facie the 'new body' of the novel is the first generation of the Brangwens, Tom and Lydia."[7] In other words, Lawrence transcended his own mood and the war atmosphere and, as a result, added the most vital generation of Brangwens and the remarkable, life-affirming opening passage.

Affirming the value of life is typical of Lawrence, although he had his dark moods and is even famous for them. He also wrote convincingly about the destructive elements in life and human nature. He was often vital and enthusiastic, however. Even as a boy his zest for life and capacity for fun caused friends and neighbors to look forward to his visits. As a man he did many things enthusiastically. He played charades, made dresses for little girls and gowns for women, fished with the peasants in Italy, wove a straw hat, and made a game out of doing the dishes. It should come as no surprise, then, that even Lawrence's mother-in-law found him lovable. He was, despite his dark moods, often positive in his approach to life and to writing about life.

In keeping with this trait, Lawrence criticized defeatism and nihilism in his contemporaries and in the characters he created for his fiction. In

1912, for example, he wrote that he hated Arnold Bennett's "resignation"[8] and could not forgive "Conrad for being so sad and for giving in."[9] Two years later, in his *Study of Thomas Hardy*, he criticized both Hardy and Tolstoy for deciding in advance that their best characters had to suffer defeat. And, as late as 1928, he criticized Connie Chatterley's bleak view of life in the early sections of *Lady Chatterley's Lover*. Despite the war and his own bouts with tuberculosis at irregular intervals, Lawrence did not believe that nihilism was inevitable. Like Nietzsche, he took a stand against nihilism. As a result, his latest works, including the poems he wrote as he was dying, are often uplifting. And in his novels his strongest characters do not give up.

As he contemplated revising and expanding *The Rainbow*, Lawrence began his study of Hardy, whose characters do give up, "out of sheer rage"[10] over the war. Written entirely during the fall of 1914, the book covers many subjects but often focuses on Hardy.[11] According to Lawrence, Hardy's best characters are "aristocrats," that is, unique, sensitive individuals who "have not been bound by the conventional morality."[12] As an artist, Hardy's tendency is to side with these unique individuals, but he arranges their defeat. Failure and misery are not inevitable in the lives of exceptional people, however, so Hardy's great novels are spoiled a bit. Lawrence believes that the novelist had to "go against himself"[13] to make sure that his aristocrats would eventually succumb.

Revising *The Rainbow* with his study of Hardy fresh in mind, Lawrence did not go against himself. Admittedly, he devoted a great deal of space to Ursula, who is tempted to succumb by becoming defeatist or at least conventional and near the end of the novel begins to think that "she would write to Skrebensky, that she would go out to him, and marry him, and live simply as a good wife to him,"[14] but she does not succumb. Although her relationship with Skrebensky is reductive and is, therefore, partially a failure, at the same time it is partially a success. It is a necessary part of that struggle into being that everyone must experience to become a complete human being.

Lawrence learned something about the need to struggle into being by studying Hardy's defeated aristocrats. He learned even more because he struggled with Frieda as he was revising *Sons and Lovers* and writing the many versions of *The Rainbow*. (In earlier versions it was called "The Sisters" and "The Wedding Ring.") But this novel about the Brangwens should not be read as autobiography, for Lawrence worked steadily "away from autobiographical material" as he wrote the various drafts, and the final draft, the one called *The Rainbow*, "was to take him further still."[15] Yet the struggle with Frieda is part of the background of the novel; it helped to shape all drafts of *The Rainbow* by helping Lawrence to understand male-female relationships. So a consideration of the Frieda-Lawrence struggle contributes to an understanding of the novel.

Although Lawrence eloped with Frieda across the English Channel on 3 May 1912, he did not marry her until 13 July 1914, eleven weeks after her divorce became final. Meanwhile, Lawrence and Frieda had to deal with the agony of Frieda's separation from her children, the cost of the divorce, and the knowledge that they had hurt Frieda's husband. Then, too, there was the clash of their two strong personalities. This clash is the subject of *Look! We Have Come Through!*, an autobiographical volume of poems that Lawrence began as early as May 1912 and did not complete until October 1917. As the title suggests, Frieda and Lawrence did come through eventually. By 3 April 1914 Lawrence could say, "Frieda and I are really very deeply happy."[16] Earlier, however, while he was working feverishly on what became *The Rainbow*, the struggle was often intense and sometimes debilitating. Accordingly, the earlier poems stress Lawrence's dejection, his fear of losing Frieda, and his love-hate conflict, but the poems in general stress a longing for equilibrium and a desire to build a life with Frieda. Ultimately, the lovers succeed. As Lawrence says in the brief "Argument" at the beginning of the volume, they "transcend into some condition of blessedness."[17] So after an intense struggle the value of the struggle is affirmed.

This affirmation appears in *The Rainbow*. As Lawrence intended, Skrebensky gives Ursula the experience she needs before she meets Rupert Birkin in *Women in Love*. Partly because of this experience she is able to resist being conventional. After all, Skrebensky is a good "catch," and she might have married him or someone just like him. But Lawrence does not force Ursula to become one of the trivial "social beings"[18] he found in the novels of a contemporary, John Galsworthy. Instead, he lets her respond to what she experiences within herself so that she has a chance to discover that neither Skrebensky nor someone like him is right for her. At the same time, she becomes aware of a morality greater than society's morality, a morality more basic than convention: a "primal morality."

Studying Shakespeare, Sophocles, Tolstoy and, in particular, Hardy, Lawrence discovered what he called "some primal morality"[19] in their works. In his own best novels this same morality exists. Heeding it, his characters, like Hardy's aristocrats, sometimes "explode out of the convention."[20] Out of the convention they have a problem: how to survive and, upon surviving, how to continue to grow. Furthermore, when they cannot rely on convention and the community, they may be free, but they have no direction. Ursula, for example, waits for "a new creation" only to discover that she has landed on the shores of "the unknown, the unexplored, the undiscovered" (494). She discovers, too, that she is alone; her family and the community cannot steer her into the future, so she has to rely on herself. She has to create her own religion.

Reading Hardy prepared Lawrence to develop as a great writer, but it did not help him to face the world once he had exploded out of convention. Here Nietzsche, the great nineteenth-century German philosopher, provided help. Admittedly, Lawrence differs from Nietzsche and even rejected some of the philosopher's views, but both men believe that the individual has to develop his own religion in the modern world. Commenting on this as a young man, Lawrence wrote to his friend, the Reverend Robert Reid: "A man has no religion who has not slowly and painfully gathered one together, adding to it, shaping it; and one's religion is never complete and final, it seems, but must always be undergoing modification."[21] In Lawrence's novels, as in Nietzsche's philosophy, religion is "always . . . undergoing modification." Beginning with *The White Peacock,* his first novel, Lawrence presents the bare outline of an ethic that is the basis of the religion that Don Ramón preaches in the 1926 novel *The Plumed Serpent.* In *The Rainbow* he is still trying to articulate his view, that is, he is trying to discover a creed to live by. To accomplish this he reviews the history of the family, which is so often the source of the individual's beliefs. He discovers the dissolution of the family and "the dissolution of a community whose values, even as these pass away, the author neither rejects nor ignores but seeks to understand and somehow for his characters' sake, to transcend."[22] In the absence of community values the characters, as individuals, must seek their own.

In *The Rainbow* Ursula must seek new values because she cannot learn what she needs to know from her family or the community. Her grandparents (Tom and Lydia) have a good marriage, and Ursula talks to Lydia about her two husbands and her adventures as a girl in Poland. But Ursula cannot become another Lydia. The family and the community have changed. As a result, Ursula's opportunities and disadvantages are not the same as Lydia's. As "the first complete modern woman, totally dispossessed and therefore totally explorative,"[23] she must seek answers within herself. To be explorative, she must have experiences, even conventional ones.

In one way she is like Sue Bridehead, a character in Hardy's last novel, *Jude the Obscure*. Sue is *intellectually* unconventional. But, according to Lawrence, Sue "wanted to live partially, in the consciousness, in the mind only. She wanted no experience in the senses, she wished only to know."[24] As a result, she fails to become a complete person and turns out to be *morally* very conventional. In contrast, Ursula indulges herself in sense experiences, even to excess, and explores the world, yet she remains dissatisfied. Briefly, she considers being promiscuous: "As an end in itself, I could love a hundred men, one after the other," she says. "Why should I end with a Skrebensky?" (475). But she also has "a yearning for something unknown" (478). Lawrence does not permit her to find an easy solution and certainly does not insist that she succumb, because unlike Hardy and like Nietzsche, Lawrence wants to present an individual who gradually discovers her own religion.

The process of discovery is not complete in *The Rainbow*. Anticipating this, Lawrence divided his novel into two volumes in January 1915. The first is *The Rainbow*; the second is *Women in Love*.

In the second volume Ursula meets Rupert Birkin and continues with him her struggle into being. This struggle takes place during the war, but the war is never mentioned. Yet the novel is, as Lawrence says, "purely destructive."[25] It is also a disturbing and brilliant account of the wartime mood and, at the same time, a reminder of the possibilities of growth for the individual during the worst of times.

But first there is *The Rainbow,* a novel written in reaction against those who convince themselves that life is inherently tragic.

Chapter 2

The Importance of the Work

Lawrence knew that *The Rainbow* was an important novel. He also knew that it differed from his earlier novels in style and form. As he revised and expanded it, he made a conscious effort to stop writing in the style of *Sons and Lovers*. Deliberately and consciously, he gave his story of the Brangwens "a new beginning—a new basis altogether."[1] The novel was so unique that it baffled Lawrence himself, causing him to admit that it seemed "like a novel in a foreign language."[2] But when Methuen rejected it, he remained confident, for he knew that his great book would eventually matter to people.

As an account of successive generations of Brangwens, *The Rainbow* reveals the significance of the great changes that have occurred so quickly within society. In particular, it stresses changes in male-female relationships and the individual's connection with the family and the larger group called, for convenience' sake, society. The novel also focuses sharply on the inner changes in the individual during the twentieth century. It is a story rich in insights into the problem of living in a rapidly changing world.

Lawrence had to discover a new way of presenting and assessing his characters as modern people. Writing to his friend Edward Garnett, he said that the "old stable ego of the character"[3] had no place in his novels, and he refused to concentrate entirely on people who were mere social beings. Intent on presenting the very souls of his characters, he could not rely exclusively on tradition or learn from his contemporaries. He had to find a way of presenting the unconscious lives of his characters.

To understand Lawrence's approach to creating characters it is necessary to grasp his starting point: "The visible world is not true. The invisible world is true and real. One must live and work from that."[4] Accordingly, Lawrence plays down the importance of what is external, for example, clothing, body types, hair color, and jewelry. Rejecting these trappings, he stresses what a character is essentially, that is, intrinsically, on the inside. In presenting a woman, for example, he is not interested in what she looks like or what she wears or even what she feels. Although he sometimes describes her—she may have blue eyes and wear yellow stockings—physical descriptions are used mainly to suggest what she is or is not like on the inside.

Skrebensky, for example, does not concern himself with his inner life. Focusing on what he is as a social being, he regards himself as a social type: an Englishman and a soldier. His uniform matters to him; he believes he has a duty to that abstraction called the nation. Connecting with the physical world through the senses only, he seeks and experiences pleasure, but he behaves as if he has no inner life; he ignores the unconscious, which can be experienced but cannot be seen or known consciously. As a result, he soon has "no being, no contents" and is "without life or being" (458).

Emphasizing that Ursula has an inner life that is real and important, Lawrence writes: "That which she was, positively, was dark and unrevealed." Then, too, he describes her as a person who is constantly changing, like a seed, and is different in "every phase" (437). Even in the last chapter of the novel she continues to evolve as an individual. Lawrence describes a deep, internal change that releases new life within her. As a result, the seed that is buried within her hard, conventional self can grow and, like a burgeoning kernel, can thrust forth a "powerful shoot" (493). The evolution makes the results of new life (the shoot) visible, but the "real" changes take place inside and cannot be seen with the naked eye.

To record the inner development of people who are constantly changing, Lawrence had to develop a new form for the novel. He voiced his objection to "all rules of construction," because they "hold good only for novels which are copies of other novels."[5] Referring to his manuscript, he warned Edward Garnett not to "look for the development of the novel to follow the lines of certain characters: the characters fall into the form of some other rhythmic form."[6] Intent on presenting the modern, dissolving family and community and the inner lives of his characters, he could not imitate his predecessors. Lawrence had to be innovative.

With regard to the form of *The Rainbow*, he is certainly innovative. According to one critic, Lawrence's novel about the Brangwens is "open,"[7] that is, the events in the novel do not converge on a conventional ending such as a death or a wedding (both of which signal an end to something). Instead, Anna's marriage occurs "directly in the middle of her story,"[8] and at the end Ursula does *not* marry Skrebensky. Furthermore, the ending is really a new beginning; there is a "new germination" (494), and everything is expanding. It is "the unknown, the unexplored, the undiscovered" (494) that matters. Then, too, Lawrence prepares the reader for the open ending early in the novel. When Ursula begins to react against her family and, later, explores "the man's world," she begins a journey that has no end. At times she rests, but "she must walk for the rest of her life" (491). When Lawrence wrote the last words of *The Rainbow*, he did not write a conclusion; instead, he created an opening into *Women in Love* wherein the kernel, having burst in Ursula, continues to grow.

Ursula draws attention to how different Lawrence's novel is from Hardy's *Jude the Obscure*, published two decades earlier, because she continues to grow. In the preface to *Jude* Hardy calls Sue Bridehead "the intellectualized, emancipated bundle of nerves that modern conditions were producing."[9] Ursula, too, is modern, but she is not nervous. Her story is later than Sue's and very much like that of many modern people. Seeking fulfillment, Ursula must consider career, marriage, motherhood, and promiscuity and, possibly, must reject all of them. Her grandparents had a good marriage in a solid community, her parents managed to cope with marriage in a changing community, and she herself has a love affair in a changed community. Although she is her grandmother's granddaughter and her father's daughter, she cannot look back because she is also unique and lives in a unique world.

It is this uniqueness, along with the uniqueness of form and characterization, that makes *The Rainbow* an important work.

Chapter 3

Critical Reception

As Lawrence wrote and rewrote *The Rainbow,* he anticipated the confusion and outrage that lay ahead. He used unusual words to describe his own novel: "weird," "queer," "futuristic." Nevertheless, he worked intensely and consciously at making his story of the Brangwens original. Deliberately, he contrasted it to *Sons and Lovers;* the style, the approach to character, and the form of the book would be new, he vowed. He even promised to dispense with the stable, traditional character.[1] So he expected confusion and knew that outrage was a good possibility. "But nobody will ever dare to publish it," he wrote in a letter.[2] Quite simply, he was convinced that people would object to the "morals" of his strange and beautiful novel.

From the very beginning people did object to the novel's morals. The earliest reviews were often blatantly hostile. But then there were a few concessions. Some reviewers found bits of beauty in the prose. One even found "innumerable fine things," but he joined the majority when he referred to the rest of the novel as "morbid" and "insane."[3] Other critics were even more antipathetic: one called the novel "an orgie of sexiness";[4] another said that it had "no right to exist."[5] Catherine Carswell, a Lawrence sympathizer, stood apart from the crowd. Writing in the

Glasgow Herald, she said that she liked the book and ranked it "with the best work done by great novelists in any age,"[6] but her unsigned review cost her her job. Clearly, people found *The Rainbow* offensive.

Those who disliked Lawrence's novel did, at times, cite what they regarded as stylistic flaws and artistic weaknesses. For example, they objected to Lawrence's use of repetition and his failure to write a conclusive ending. Then, too, because the novel is innovative, they were genuinely baffled by it. Nevertheless, they understood enough to react to the novel's subject matter. They found it obscene.

The government had the same reaction. Supporting the hostile reviewers, public officials charged Lawrence with obscenity under the Obscene Publications Act of 1857. Methuen had to explain why all copies of the book should not be destroyed. And although several people did come to Lawrence's defense, they were not persuasive enough to rescue the book. As the *Times* reported on 15 November 1915, "the magistrate ordered that the copies should be destroyed and that the defendants should pay £10 10s. costs."[7]

In retrospect, it is easy to understand what offended so many people: Anna dancing naked in her bedroom, the lesbian encounters between Ursula and Winifred, the "reductive" lovemaking of Skrebensky and Ursula—and Lawrence's portrayal of the military. In this 1915 novel Lawrence does not take an antiwar stand, but he does, through Ursula, present a criticism of Skrebensky's nationalism and a dislike of soldiers. In a wartime atmosphere such views are dangerous and offensive. So it is not surprising that the very hostile reviews of *The Rainbow* were inspired very little by the literary quality of the novel and a great deal by personal feelings. Quite simply, people objected to the novel's morals.

This reaction is not surprising because Lawrence consciously sought to discover new, and thus threatening, values as he wrote. Like Blake and Nietzsche before him, he was an original thinker and a rebel or, as Eugene Goodheart says, a tablet breaker.[8] At the same time, Lawrence deliberately provoked his readers. He wanted them to be affected by his prose because he wanted them to change. As a result, he made his method as important as his message. He used a style that makes responding passively to his provocative themes and scenes difficult.

When provoked, readers nearly always take sides. Fortunately, F. R. Leavis took Lawrence's side, but even this great and influential critic was baffled at first. In an essay published in the year of Lawrence's death (1930), Leavis admitted that he found it difficult to keep the characters in the fiction apart and felt that *The Lost Girl* was Lawrence's best novel. At this early date, he even had reservations about Lawrence's style. But he also recognized Lawrence's genius and admired the "splendid artistic maturity" of *Lady Chatterley's Lover*.[9] So it is not surprising that in 1955 he placed Lawrence in "the great tradition" of English novelists and, in doing so, made Lawrence a novelist everyone had to take seriously.

In the appendix to *D. H. Lawrence: Novelist* (1955), "Mr. Eliot and Lawrence," Leavis defends Lawrence against T. S. Eliot's charge of ignorance and stresses Lawrence's wholeness, vitality, and judgment—that is, he argues that Lawrence was a healthy, vigorous, educated, and disciplined writer.[10] Because Eliot had such prestige as a poet and critic, Leavis's defense was necessary even twenty-five years after Lawrence's death. The "tablet-breaker" was still threatening.

But Leavis does more than defend Lawrence against indignant readers. In the chapter "Lawrence and Tradition: *The Rainbow*" he places Lawrence in the tradition of George Eliot, the great Victorian novelist, and draws attention to both the form and the content of Lawrence's novel. He does not ignore what he regards as weaknesses: Ursula's "too long-drawn-out" affair with Skrebensky and the weak, inconclusive ending.[11] Leavis says that "in an important sense, *The Rainbow* is not a finished work." But he also stresses Lawrence's strengths: his originality, his interest in the individual's potential for self-realization, his sense of "the oneness of life," and his genius as a technical innovator.[12] And, always, he regards Lawrence as important, so he takes him seriously on a variety of other subjects: those "delicate and complex responsive relations" that are so very important to the individual, fulfillment, Lawrence's religious nature, Ursula's development as an individual, and Skrebensky's "inadequacy as a lover."[13] In brief, by being thorough and perceptive, Leavis makes it impossible after 1955 for any serious student of the novel to ignore Lawrence.

While Leavis was writing *D. H. Lawrence: Novelist*, Mark Spilka was writing *The Love Ethic of D. H. Lawrence* (1955), which is still one of the finest and most perceptive studies of Lawrence. As the title suggests, Spilka concentrates on Lawrence's view of love. Like Leavis, he regards Lawrence as a religious writer, but he goes beyond Leavis when he states that "love is a religious experience" for Lawrence.[14] In discussing Lawrence's special response to love, Spilka uses the term "love ethic," by which he means "radical commitment to spontaneous life, and to 'phallic marriage' as the fount of life itself."[15] But love for married couples and for unmarried lovers in Lawrence's novels is not solely physical. When Spilka explores the love ethic, he underscores the connection that exists between the sensual and the spiritual. Commenting specifically on *The Rainbow*, he says that "there is a decided connection . . . between satisfaction of the deepest sensual self and a more spiritual form of satisfaction." Whereas the first two generations of Brangwens are only partially successful in seeking fulfillment, "Ursula Brangwen fares better." Rejecting "the conventional frame of life" and fighting "all her major battles *before* marriage," she eventually finds herself "through marriage with Rupert Birkin" in *Women in Love*.[16] In brief, through her relationship with a man, she achieves completeness and wholeness.

Even today Leavis and Spilka are reference points for people who study Lawrence. What they said in the fifties is still, in large part, valid. Occasionally, however, there is a turning point or at least a new emphasis in Lawrence criticism. One such turning point occurred in 1959 when Marvin Mudrick published what is possibly the best essay on *The Rainbow*. Called "The Originality of *The Rainbow*," the essay itself is original. Clearly it echoes Leavis and is indebted to Spilka, but it stresses the revolutionary rather than the traditional aspects of Lawrence's novel. According to Mudrick, *The Rainbow* is revolutionary in two important ways: "it is the first English novel to record the normality and significance of physical passion; and it is the only English novel to record, with a prophetic awareness of consequences, the social revolution whereby Western man lost his sense of community and men—more especially, women—learned, if they could, that there is no help any longer except in the individual and in his capacity for a passional life."[17] Certainly Mudrick does not disprove either Leavis or Spilka. Writing about *The*

Rainbow, he is aware of Lawrence's debt to the past and even follows Leavis's lead by studying each of the three generations of Brangwens. At the same time, however, Mudrick stresses Lawrence's departure from traditional writers such as Henry Fielding, an eighteenth-century novelist whose concern is manners and morals. He also dwells on Ursula's need to rely on herself as an individual and to learn from experience because society's "sanctions and prohibitions" are passé.[18] Thus he adds a new dimension to the growing body of serious Lawrence criticism.

Largely because of Leavis, Spilka, and Mudrick Lawrence was regarded as a major writer in the sixties, but he was not yet considered entirely respectable. To the general reader he was still known primarily as the author of the infamous *Lady Chatterley's Lover.* Besides, he had written other "offensive" works such as *The Plumed Serpent* and *The Man Who Died,* and unflattering stories about his private life circulated among literary gossips. As a result, people were suspicious of him and could not resist the temptation to respond to him as a personality rather than a writer. Even in scholarly works, normally detached critics attacked his character and accused him of holding the wrong views on such subjects as women, Christianity, power, and aggression. And many, friends and foes alike, believed that *Sons and Lovers* was his last well-constructed novel.

In 1966 Keith Sagar tried to set the record straight by writing *The Art of D. H. Lawrence,* a book about Lawrence's originality as a constructor of novels. In this important study Sagar is indebted to both Leavis and Mudrick. Although he asserts that "Lawrence's beliefs have the authentic discipline of a great religion,"[19] he also reacts against Leavis and tries to go beyond him in his own assessment of the novels as works of art. He emphasizes that Leavis, like T. S. Eliot and J. M. Murry (Lawrence's friend, the model for Gerald Crich in *Women in Love,* and the author of one of the first books about Lawrence), missed the point of what Lawrence was trying to do—namely, ignore the rules that govern the construction of conventional novels. Sagar believes that Lawrence was not indifferent to artistry; instead, he sought the "appropriate form" for each of his novels, that is, the form that would enable him to discover a morality within his novels.[20] The results of Lawrence's originality were novels that had form, but not what Eliot, Murry, and Leavis expected to find.

Stressing Lawrence's artistry, Sagar contributed to the building of Lawrence's reputation as a serious writer. Stressing Lawrence's originality, he persuaded critics and general readers alike to reconsider remarks about carelessly constructed portions of "major" works such as *The Rainbow*. And, by acknowledging the religious element in Lawrence's works, he reinforced the views of both Leavis and Spilka.

Of course, Spilka, Leavis, and Sagar were not the only people to write about Lawrence's religious nature; they were not even the first. As early as 1951 Father Tiverton commented on Lawrence's affinity with "the Christian view of sex" in *Lady Chatterley's Lover*.[21] Others followed suit. By 1963 the emphasis on Lawrence's affinity with Christianity caused Eugene Goodheart to remind readers that "the essential animus" in Lawrence's work is "averse to Christianity."[22] Nevertheless, as a thinker, moralist, and artist, Lawrence was becoming respectable. In particular, *The Rainbow* and *Women in Love* were becoming established as modern classics, discussed by virtually everyone interested in the novel. It seemed, for a while, as if nothing new would be said about them.

But Colin Clarke contributed something new in 1969. In *River of Dissolution: D. H. Lawrence and English Romanticism* he tries to rescue Lawrence from the moralists and to change the direction of Lawrence scholarship. To accomplish this, he discusses corruption and degradation in Lawrence's fiction, but he discovers a new significance in this old subject.

Clarke begins by acknowledging that there is "corruption" in the Ursula-Skrebensky relationship. He discusses the "reductive behavior" of all three generations of Brangwens. In contrast to earlier critics, however, he finds "a virtue in degradation." Without claiming that degradation (or reduction) is good, he maintains that it leads to something good. Accordingly, he describes Skrebensky's sensuality as "at once reductive, regressive, a breaking down . . . and a release into infinity." In brief, Clarke stresses that love is a process in *The Rainbow*, that the process includes both destructive and creative elements, and that lovers must accept and express both elements because "sensual ecstasy has its roots in corruption."[23]

In his treatment of dissolution Clarke teaches people to consider and take seriously what has generally been perceived as ugly and undesirable, even in the greatest Lawrence novels. Thus, he enhances Lawrence's reputation and at the same time forces some revisions in the interpretations of the characters. For example, he exonerates Skrebensky to some extent and places more responsibility on Ursula for her failures. He also helps to explain the "shape" and style of *The Rainbow*. Acknowledging that there is repetition in the novel, he relates that repetition to Lawrence's purpose in writing the book, which he sees as Lawrence's exploration of the recurrence of the reductive process and his presentation of "the full cumulative significance of the discoveries made in the course of that exploration." Thus what seems to be only repetition adds up to "a richness of meaning."[24]

Defending and explaining Lawrence's presentation of corruption, Clarke convinces the reader that apparent weaknesses in *The Rainbow* are in reality contributions to the novel's artistry and complexity. He helps to destroy the image of Lawrence as an untutored genius and careless, although gifted, artist. Lawrence still has detractors; even that beautiful book called *The Plumed Serpent* is regarded with suspicion and is sometimes savagely attacked. Nevertheless, after Clarke published *The River of Dissolution* in the last year of the sixties, many Lawrence critics had to pause and reconsider the value of the "odious" portions of Lawrence's works, including *The Rainbow*. After all, if there is "an essential life-energy" in corruption,[25] to reject what is odious is to reject life itself.

With Clarke's book behind them, critics of the seventies and eighties wanted to get at the essential Lawrence, so they broadened the base of Lawrence criticism. At the same time, when they wrote about the novels, they focused on two main subjects: form and content. In *D. H. Lawrence* (1973) Frank Kermode writes about both subjects and stresses the need to understand that the metaphysic of *The Rainbow* is "part of the tissue of the narrative and the rhetoric, which are not subdued."[26]

But also is 1973 Scott Sanders published *D. H. Lawrence: The World of the Five Major Novels.* In this interesting and challenging book Sanders is interested in the individual but is far more interested in the individual's relation to society. Consistent with this thesis, he argues that "the antagonism between social and natural man" is "a dominant feature of Lawrence's thought" beginning with *The Rainbow.* Developing his argument, Sanders discusses a dichotomy that he finds in Lawrence's major novels: the social self (which is false) and the natural self (which is creative and spontaneous). In *The Rainbow* it is evident that Lawrence is dissatisfied with society, for he "invariably" presents nature as more powerful and appealing than society. Then, too, beginning with "the latter chapters of *The Rainbow . . .* his characters are in constant flight from society."[27] *The Rainbow* is, then, a novel about the broad context of man's existence, but it also includes the failure of individuals.

As a study of the failure of modern people in the social world, Sanders's book is not primarily psychological (although it contains some fine psychological insights); nevertheless, it anticipates a series of psychological studies that appeared in the seventies and eighties. One of the most important of these is Marguerite Beede Howe's *The Art of the Self in D. H. Lawrence* (1977). Howe's contention is that Lawrence is mostly concerned with "identity, and the fragmented self." She perceives the conflict between "self and Not-me" as inherent in all the "modern relationships" that can be found in Lawrence's fiction, including *The Rainbow.*[28] She alludes to Ursula's ability to "engulf" her lover, to Birkin's "inverting the proposition" and engulfing Ursula, and to Ursula's "potential danger" as a lover. In brief, Howe stresses that "Lawrence's new idea of personality [is] the basis of *The Rainbow,*" namely, "that we have a social self and an essential one." She also strongly suggests that relationships in the novel are reductive. Thus Skrebensky is a hollow man and Ursula herself "is at least partly responsible" for his condition.[29]

Daniel Schneider's *D. H. Lawrence: The Artist As Psychologist* (1984) continues the series of psychological studies. At the same time, it is an attempt to rescue Lawrence from reductive criticism. As the title of this difficult and valuable book suggests, Schneider regards Lawrence as a psychologist as well as an artist. Therefore, he includes an entire chapter on Lawrence's theory of the unconscious. Nevertheless, he does not concentrate on the connection between Lawrence and Freud; instead, he stresses the materialism of Lawrence and links him with Schopenhauer and Nietzsche. He expresses his belief that a study of man's deepest motives does not result in a denigration of man; rather, it reveals that man's deepest motives are religious or creative.[30]

Schneider admits that Lawrence and many of his main characters have not entirely found themselves by 1915 despite the novelist's study of man's deepest motives. In both *The Rainbow* and *Women in Love,* "The males, insufficiently active or conscious, are unable to find a purpose beyond that of serving women; they are insufficiently differentiated, only half-created, half-developed. The females, unable to live with men who have no purpose and no real courage to adventure into the unknown, become erratic, seeking fulfillment in a freedom that is irresponsible and chaotic. Only Ursula and Rupert Birkin in *Women in Love* find the right union and right balance." Yet, according to Schneider, men and women in Lawrence's fiction can, like Ursula and Birkin, become "distinct sexual beings and discover wholeness of being in their union." So whereas Lawrence does at times present his characters' limitations, he also emphasizes their quest for wholeness.[31]

Schneider's study of Lawrence the psychologist is important, as is his later book, *The Consciousness of D. H. Lawrence: An Intellectual Biography* (1986). Both books emphasize Lawrence's health and vitality. Schneider says that Lawrence "must celebrate life at all costs."[32] Such a reminder is timely even now, because some critics still write reductively about Lawrence. Judith Ruderman, for example, stresses Lawrence's fixation at the pre-oedipal stage of his psychosexual development in *D. H. Lawrence and the Devouring Mother: The Search for a Patriarchal Ideal of Leadership* (1984). Using psychoanalytic theory, Ruderman often has excellent insights into the novels and tales. Then, too, she has a fine chapter on Lawrence's two psychoanalytic essays, which are retrospective comments on *The Rainbow* and *Women in Love.* But she assumes there is a great deal of autobiography in the novels and, consequently, reduces everything to "Lawrence's own mother fixation and the nature of the earliest, pre-genital relationship between all mothers and their children," which are, she says, "the central concerns of Lawrence's career." Thus she stresses Lawrence's (rather than his characters') dependence on women, his need to dominate strong females, and his ambivalence and misogyny. Therefore she ignores the health and vitality that Schneider finds in Lawrence's books, or she simply does not believe that they are there. And whereas she focuses on the so-called leadership period—that is, on *Aaron's Rod* and the works that immediately follow—her contention is that Lawrence never did overcome his mother fixation. Thus her comments apply—or are meant to apply—to all of Lawrence's works.[33]

A review of Lawrence criticism reveals the provocative nature of the ongoing debate over *The Rainbow.* The debate will continue, for the recent psychological studies are not summaries but challenges that require a response. Nevertheless, a composite of Lawrence the writer is emerging: He is an artist of religious intensity, a first-rate thinker, an innovator, and a psychologist. Then, too, when critics focus on *The Rainbow,* they feel compelled to consider certain subjects: the three generations of Brangwens, the dissolving community, the relation of man to society, the need for the individual to discover a religion, the Ursula-Skrebensky relationship, and the "inconclusive" ending. At the same time, however, there are subjects that have not been adequately explored. For example, very little has been said about Lawrence's handling of point of view or the positive values he finds in aggression. So the criticism, while still evolving, is invaluable; without it, the general reader and the specialist alike would get lost in the beautiful and bewildering world of *The Rainbow.*

A Reading

Chapter 4

Ursula: At the Edge of Darkness

Ursula Brangwen has to discover her own religion. As she passes "from girlhood towards womanhood," she realizes that her old religion "was not true—at least, for this present-day life of ours." In the modern world, there can be "no Feeding of the Five Thousand," she believes. "And the girl had come to the point where she held that that which one cannot experience in daily life is not true for oneself" (283). Deprived of religion she misses a traditional means of comfort and value.

She is also deprived of other traditional sources of meaning and value, specifically, love and family. She experiments with love and finds that it gives pleasure; it even satisfies her bodily at times. But modern love—or what is called love—is too personal, that is, it is of the person or body only, so it does not lead anywhere. Realizing that love results in disillusionment, Ursula is forced to admit that she does not care about or value love (475).

Nor does she care about family and babies. In contrast to her mother and grandmother, she is "in revolt against babies and muddled domesticity" (275), so when she sees Rubens's *Fecundity*, a painting filled with naked babies, she shudders and begins to abhor the word "fecundity." Also, within her own family she has experienced the "bedlam" that results when there are many children in the house, so it does not matter to her that her mother flourishes in the midst of all the noise and confusion. As far as she knows consciously, she wants nothing to do with domestic life. She believes she is in revolt against convention itself.

In some ways, Ursula is in revolt, but she is also very conventional as a girl. When she rejects her parents' values, is excited by a car, and falls in love with a soldier, she is no rebel. Then, too, when she is in love, she is typical rather than unique. Putting her ring in Rhine wine, she drinks from the glass. She also gives Skrebensky her photograph and accepts sweets from him. So, to the casual observer, when she has her first affair with Anton, Ursula seems to be an ordinary teenager, yet she is far from ordinary by the end of the novel. As a young woman who changes in her soul and reacts to those changes by making the unconscious conscious, she is unique.

Then, too, she lives in a unique era and cannot look to the past to determine how to live in the present. She often reacts against tradition and the rules that bind her. At the same time, the past is a strong force that shapes and forms her and is part of what she is in the present, even as she resists and rebels against the past. For example, the fairy tales she loves as a child determine, to an extent, how she perceives her lover Skrebensky and what she expects of love. Her close relationship with her father, Will, has a similar effect on her. Furthermore, she resembles her grandfather, Tom, who is developed in feeling and is "sensitive to the atmosphere around him" (16) and, like the Brangwen women who aspire to something beyond themselves, she wants something from life but cannot articulate what she wants. So Ursula may rebel against the past and reject its values, but she is also a product of that past.

Nevertheless, she lives in the present and wants satisfaction in her own lifetime. Her grandparents and great-grandparents had what she wants. For example, Alfred and his wife, the unnamed woman from Heanor, had a solid marriage and, later, Tom and Lydia know "an inner reality, a logic of the soul, which connected her with him" (41), but, as the past blends into the present in *The Rainbow*, relations between the sexes become more and more strained, and marriage becomes a duel. Thus Ursula's parents, Anna and Will, have a less satisfying marriage than their parents, what Mudrick refers to as the "imperfect truce."[1] As a result, Ursula cannot assume that marriage and love will give meaning to her life or make her satisfied. Unlike Alfred and his wife, she and a man cannot be "two very separate beings, vitally connected, knowing nothing of each other, yet living in their separate ways from one root" (13). Too much has changed.

Some of the change is visible. For example, the Midland Railway and a colliery invade the meadows of the Marsh Farm where the Brangwens live, and desecrate the land. As a result, the community is disrupted and man's solid connection with the fecund earth is broken. As the outside world encroaches on the private lives of the characters, they are affected inside; they become discontented and yearn for something that is not in their blood. One Brangwen woman, for example, is attracted to "the far-off world of cities and governments and the active scope of man, the magic land to her, where secrets were made known and desires fulfilled" (9). Then, too, Alfred's eldest son anticipates Ursula's restlessness by running off to sea, and Ursula's Uncle Tom wanders the earth until he finally settles down on the scarred ground near Wiggiston. Affected by changes in the community and in the land itself, the characters in *The Rainbow* feel more and more alienated from other people and the rich earth.

Despite their alienation, most of the characters marry eventually, and Ursula could follow suit, for in *The Rainbow* marriage is a means of avoiding responsibility for one's own life. But it also offers pleasure and satisfaction. To illustrate this point, Lawrence records an ordinary family scene late in the novel. Ursula's family has just moved from "Cossethay, where the children had all been born" (419), and are in their new home near Willey Green, on the edge of the colliery district: "Everything was at sixes and sevens. But a fire was made in the kitchen, the hearth-rug put down, the kettle set on the hob, and Mrs. Brangwen began towards sunset to prepare the first meal. Ursula and Gudrun were slaving in the bedrooms, candles were rushing about. Then from the kitchen came the smell of ham and eggs and coffee, and in the gaslight, the scrambled meal began. The family seemed to huddle together like a little camp in a strange place" (426). In this conventional setting, the Brangwens experience warmth, comfort, and a jumbled security as they anticipate "the scrambled meal," so the promise of marriage (and family) is kept. But the noise and closeness are a warning against marriage for people like Ursula. Thus, when she rejects Anthony Scofield's marriage proposal in chapter 14 she makes what is the right decision for her, for marriage with Anthony implies children and Ursula is not comfortable with the responsibility of babies, as is evident when Lawrence concludes his description of the Brangwens at supper with the reminder that "Ursula felt a load of responsibility upon her, caring for the half-little ones" (426). Unlike Anna, she cannot settle for staying at home as a married woman.

In retrospect, it is obvious that marriage and children are not enough for many of the characters who are younger than Alfred and his wife. There is something incomplete, something unresolved, in persons such as Winifred Inger and Maggie Schofield but also in the Brangwens. For example, although Tom Brangwen prospers, remains fresh, laughs a great deal, and has blue eyes that are full of life, he is "afraid of the unknown in life" (242) and expresses some dissatisfaction. Later, his son Will spends much of his time "groping, always groping on" (418), and Uncle Tom, the globe-trotter, is a model citizen, but when he marries, "Neither marriage nor the domestic establishment meant anything to him" (352). Even Anna, who is unconventional at times and experiences great physical pleasure, has to live through other people, especially her babies. So Ursula is wise to recognize that marriage is not inevitably fulfilling. People who marry for conventional reasons limit themselves and remain dissatisfied.

Yet Lawrence was a champion of marriage. In his own life he insisted upon a formal wedding ceremony and, in a letter in which he told Frieda, "I shall love you all my life," he commented on the great thing that marriage can be: "Because it is a great thing for me to marry you, not a quick, passionate coming together. I know in my heart 'here's my marriage.' It feels rather terrible—because it is a great thing in my life—it is *my life*—I am a bit awe-inspired—I want to get used to it."[2] Then, too, although Ursula does not marry in *The Rainbow,* the novel opens up at the end and leads into *Women in Love,* where the promise of marriage is kept. In this continuation of the story of the Brangwens, Ursula meets Rupert Birkin and receives from him "the maximum of unspeakable communication in touch, dark, subtle, positively silent, a magnificent gift and give again, a perfect acceptance and yielding."[3] And Rupert Birkin, who resembles Lawrence in some ways, regards marriage with Ursula as "his resurrection and his life."[4] There is no doubt that Lawrence values marriage when the individuals involved do not marry for conventional reasons.

In *The Rainbow* Ursula seems hostile to marriage; in the next book she hesitates before she accepts Rupert, but she is reacting against what marriage has become in the modern world: a physical union and the means of having a family. So she tries alternatives to being a wife and mother: affairs with Skrebensky, a brief fling with her twenty-eight-year-old school mistress, college, and a career as a teacher. Each time she is greatly disillusioned. She is ashamed of her lesbian affair, loathes teaching unwilling students, comes to regard college as "the sham workshop" (435), and realizes that she has no connection with Anton. After a while it becomes obvious that he has been an excuse for neglecting her studies and failing her exams, so she rejects him, her education, and her career and finds herself "up against her own fate" (474). Unwilling to accept traditional values and unable to find new meaning in the world of material objects, she has two choices. Playing it safe, she can go through the motions of being conventional and remain empty or, taking a chance, she can search for new life within herself.

Searching for new life, she cannot rely on the church or be guided by its teachings, for the stories from the Bible seem inimical to her life. Thus she is forced to rely on her own troubled experiences, including her mistakes. When one of her experiences, her second affair with Skrebensky, breaks the "bonds of the world" and sets her adrift in "a new country, in a new life" (472), she realizes that she has freedom but no direction and no connection with anything. As a result, she has to do something if she wants new life. "She must modify her soul" (472).

To modify her soul, Ursula must go beyond consciousness, which Lawrence associates with light and knowing, to the unconscious, which is dark and unknown. She must do what other Brangwens are afraid to do. According to Lawrence, "no man dared even throw a firebrand into the darkness. For if he did he was jeered to death by the others, who cried 'Fool, anti-social knave, why do you disturb us with bogeys? There *is* no darkness. We move and live and have our being within the light'" (438). But, as *The Rainbow* illustrates, people are affected by the unconscious whether or not they acknowledge its existence. For example, neither Anna nor Will admits to being domineering but both try to dominate. As Lawrence says, what is "in the darkness" is "not to be denied" (438).

During her second affair with Skrebensky Ursula comes to the edge of darkness and at least peers into its heart, although doing so is not easy for her. When she first sees "the eyes of the wild beast gleaming from the darkness" (437), she is frightened and represses what she knows briefly. When Skrebensky is "helpless" and "at her mercy," she knows that she could reject him and "something would die in him," but she refuses to dwell consciously on what is happening. Instead, "all must be kept so dark, the consciousness must admit nothing" (443). Nor is this an isolated case. Reacting to what is unpleasant, Ursula often denies the darkness within herself.

At other times she wants to face the darkness; she wants to penetrate the "cold surface of consciousness" (458) and wants to go beyond herself to "something impersonal" (475). For a long time, however, she continues to dwell on what is conscious, and in doing so, she pays a price; she is revulsed by "superficial life," and her own inner life becomes "cold, dead, inert" (481). She is soon like a dead person, so she begins to struggle to make the unconscious conscious.

The Rainbow is a book about the preparations for and the very beginning of this struggle and is thus a book about Ursula. Not everyone views the book in this way. Some of the best Lawrence critics find the Ursula section weak and believe that Lawrence lost interest in it. And, certainly, the earlier sections of the novel are denser, but a dense style is not appropriate to some portions of the Ursula story, for example, her exploration of the flat world of consciousness and material objects. So the style is more fluid and less turbid when Lawrence describes Ursula's rush through the social world; this does not mean that Lawrence had no interest in Ursula's life. After all, he devoted half of his great novel to her story and continued that story in *Women in Love*. Clearly, he deemed her exploration of "superficial life" important.

At the same time, the earlier sections of the novel are important. Although different from the Ursula section, they are not separate from it. After all, Ursula was not fashioned out of a man's rib; she is what issues from generations of people interacting, making love, fighting, and having babies. Genetically, these earlier generations predetermine, to some extent, what she is like; they make her, inevitably, a Brangwen.

But she is not only a Brangwen. She also resembles her Polish grandmother and must resemble Polish people she never knew. It is impossible to sort out and analyze the mix of traits she inherits and acquires. Nevertheless, she is limited by what she is genetically. No matter how much she idealizes, she can only be herself.

According to Lawrence, a person who goes beyond knowing himself to being himself has accomplished a great deal, for there are many obstacles to self-fulfillment. In particular, everyone needs to be able to interact with other people because no one can become himself in isolation. Commenting on this in an essay called "We Need One Another," Lawrence says that "We have our very individuality in relationship,"[5] that is, we become ourselves by establishing connections with other people. Most people insist on conformity and thus impede the growth of those unique people Lawrence calls aristocrats. Thus, if Ursula wants to grow, she must adjust to the world of other people without becoming conventional. In undertaking this goal she cannot expect from the community what it gave to her grandparents: guidance and stability.

To understand Ursula, it is necessary to understand what has happened within the community, and among the earlier Brangwens. The novel, however, moves steadily toward Lawrence's main interest: Ursula. At the beginning of her story, she is a child living at home and experiencing love, frustration, and conflict and, later, she becomes involved with the outside world as a teenager. Being young and hopeful, she is often disillusioned. Near the end of the novel, when she is a young woman, she feels confined and believes she must "break out of" (493) the world. In trying to do so, she makes a mistake, for she cannot escape from the world, but she gives herself a chance to grow beyond her conventional life and her utter dependence on physical objects, which includes Anton's body. Growth is not inevitable, however, as

Lawrence suggests when he blends images of life ("root" and "new ground") with images of death and sterility ("ash" and "ashiness"). Near the end of the novel, Ursula faces a crisis. Experimenting with her life, she may destroy herself emotionally, but she may come through to "new life."

Chapter 5

Alfred's Generation:
The Importance of Surety

When Ursula begins to search for new life, she cannot know that she wants what Lawrence calls surety. Nor can she know that her great-grandparents had surety because they existed in relationship with the land, the community, and each other. This state of communion does not mean that they are not individuals; the woman from Heanor is described as "intrinsically separate" (13), for example. Nevertheless, both she and her husband derive strength from being connected with something beyond themselves. Separate but closely related, they are like two "beings" growing from "one root" (13).

Less than three pages from the end of *The Rainbow*, Lawrence comments on Ursula's progress, "She had her root in new ground" (493). The word "new" is significant and suggests that Ursula cannot live in the soil of her great-grandparents or even that of her parents. Then, too, because she has not yet established a vital connection with a man, she is a single plant growing from that root and has not matched her great-grandparents' level of personal satisfaction. Furthermore, unlike them, she is aware of a "void" between her and a man (494), a "rift" in the world, and a "space" between her and the "earth's shell" (493). Clearly, her connection with the land, the community, and a man is not the same as that of Alfred's wife. Thus, if Ursula wants to be vitally alive, she cannot merely imitate her great-grandmother. She has to find a new direction, in new soil.

The rift that Ursula is aware of did not begin to develop in her generation; it began at about the time that Alfred married the woman from Heanor. (Lawrence is not exact about chronology in the opening pages of the novel.) As a result of the rift, their children do not have their parents' surety. The oldest son runs away to sea and never returns. The second, Alfred Junior (Ursula's paternal grandfather), marries the daughter of a chemist, is respectable for a while, but eventually goes after "strange women," pursues "forbidden pleasure," and neglects his conventional wife "without a qualm" (14). The third son, Frank, becomes a butcher because he is attracted to blood and likes the sight of kidneys exposed from huge sides of beef. Like his older brother, Frank marries a docile, conventional woman; later, he becomes a heavy drinker. Alfred's two daughters become conventional in different ways. The elder, Alice, marries a collier, has a stormy marriage in nearby Ilkeston, and then moves away with her large family. Elfie, the younger daughter, remains at home, unmarried. Tom, the youngest by far, will be discussed at length in chapter 6. Tom comes closest to having his parents' surety, but he and his siblings illustrate collectively that the individual's relationship to the community is changing. The younger generation (Ursula's grandparents and their contemporaries) are no longer closely connected to other people or the land. Alienated somewhat, they aspire to social success, want what they do not have, move away from home (apparently with ease), and remain restless and dissatisfied.

In order to understand what has been lost with the passage of time, a study of Alfred and the woman from Heanor is in order. Discussed only briefly in *The Rainbow,* they have a relationship that is not perfect, but is certainly stable. She is "oddly a thing to herself . . . intrinsically separate and indifferent." As a habitual complainer, she plays no favorites and raises her voice against everybody. But nobody minds. Rather, those who hear her "feel affectionately towards her, even whilst they were irritated and impatient with her." Alfred is mortified at what she says about him, but her speech also warms "his belly with pride and male triumph." Thus, he "calmly did as he liked, laughed at her railing, excused himself in a teasing tone that she loved, followed his natural inclinations" (13). Although they subject one another to the opposition that is inevitable when strong people live side by side, each is stable enough to handle the other's moods and verbal attacks and to remain "vitally connected." Each has the stable ego that Lawrence says his readers should not look for in his novels.

Then, in about 1840, a canal is constructed that connects the new collieries nearby. After the Brangwens receive money for "this trespass across their land" (12), the "invasion" continues, but the Marsh Farm remains relatively secluded. The farm, however, is not out of touch with the desecration of the land that occurs just beyond the farm. Looking up, the Brangwens can see "the dim smoking hill of the town" (12). Without straining, they can hear "the rhythmic run of the winding engines . . ., the shrill whistle of the trains," and the "clink-clink-clink-clink-clink of empty trucks" (13). Then, too, there is odor, the "sulphurous smell of pit-refuse burning" (13). Reacting to this noise and air pollution, the Brangwens become strangers in their own land and feel alienated from the rich, life-sustaining earth.

Significantly, the "Alfred Brangwen of this period had married a woman from Heanor" before the invasion of the land began and before the farmers began to meet the "blackened colliers trooping from the pit-mouth" (13). As a result, he has the surety that is reflected in his easy bantering with his sharp-tongued wife, but his children fall victim to "all this commotion around them" (12). But they do not perceive themselves as victims; instead, they seem to crave the commotion, for the noise of the engines is "a narcotic to the brain," and the train whistle offers "pleasure" that is "fearsome" but is nevertheless pleasure (13). Later in the story the noise and ugly sights and unpleasant odors are taken for granted; they come to represent the earth. Thus Ursula moves easily from the comparatively clean and peaceful countryside to Willey Green and even to noisy Paris. For her and for the Brangwens in general the attraction to the land becomes fainter and fainter. It is no surprise, then, that Ursula does not want to work on the land or even at home; she plans to have a profession—in the city.

A characteristic of the Brangwens is that they aspire to social status beyond the position of the farmer; but for a long time, they are farmers who make a living with their hands. Working the fields, the Brangwen men can see a church tower two miles away. Mark Spilka says that the rising tower "represents an outworn form of spirituality."[1] His observation reminds us that the Brangwens are not enthusiastic about attending church and that Ursula is not able to make the church a meaningful part of her life. The Brangwens in the first chapter of *The Rainbow* are not yet indifferent to the tower, however. After looking at it and turning again to the land, they remain "aware of something" that is above and beyond them. Like Will and Ursula later, they yearn toward that something, and although they cannot say what it is, they are ready and eager and expect "something unknown" (7). While they wait, they have surety because they still feel connected to the land and to each other, and they feel the influence of religion, which is symbolized by the church tower.

At the beginning of the novel Lawrence emphasizes the close connection between the earth and the Brangwens, who are roughly contemporary with Alfred, by using the words "intercourse" and "impregnated." The Brangwens know "the intercourse between heaven and earth." Then, too, the women "look out from the heated, blind intercourse of farm-life," and the men are "impregnated with the day, cattle and earth and vegetation and the sky" (8). The bond between the Brangwens and the earth is so strong that Lawrence uses sexual terms to describe it.

The bond is so strong because without thinking about life, these early Brangwens live it. For example, they help the cows to give birth, grip their horses between their knees, and take the udders of the cows in their hands. During the day they stand in the open fields and face the sun. As a result, they actually feel "the rush of the sap in spring" (7). And, like Alfred and his wife, they are close to one another. Emphasizing this on the first page of the novel, Lawrence refers to the residents of the Marsh Farm as a group, "the Brangwens." Although they are divided into two subgroups, the women and the men, they are closely related to one another, and both groups have surety.

But then a rift occurs between the two sexes. "The women were different," says Lawrence (8), announcing that there is an opposition between men and women, an opposition that continues, in mild form, with Lydia and Tom, becomes more serious with Anna and Will, and has its culmination when Ursula "annihilates" Skrebensky. Reacting to the invasion of the outside world, the women become aware that there is something beyond the artificial boundaries of the farm. But the men remain close to the fields and continue to work because they want to, "because of the life that was in them, not for want of the money" (7). And although they are expectant, the men do not expect anything from outside the boundaries of their land. So, at the end of the day their brains are "inert" as they sit by the fire. "It was enough for the men, that the earth heaved and opened its furrows to them" (8). Living in harmony with the seasons and the rooks and the grey sky, they are "full and surcharged, their senses full fed, their faces always turned to the heat of the blood" (9).

The women know "the drowse of blood-intimacy" (8), but while the men turn inward to the land, the women look out from the life of the farm "to the spoken world" (8). As a result, they know what the men know and something more; "the woman" wants "another form of life than this, something that was not blood-intimacy" (9).

It is tempting to take sides, that is, to blame the men for being so narrow or to blame the women for being dissatisfied in the midst of prosperity. But Lawrence does not take sides or make it easy for his readers to take sides. Instead, he places the men and the women in a particular setting, creates a situation, and lets a conflict develop. During the conflict, the strengths and weaknesses of both sexes become obvious; however, neither sex monopolizes a trait. Thus, both Will and Anna are domineering, and Lydia and Tom are equally self-confident and are assertive in their own different ways.

It is obvious that Lawrence likes those individuals who, like Ursula, become self-responsible and look beyond themselves to the invisible world. Conversely, Lawrence indicates that characters who refuse to look beyond themselves are unfulfilled and incomplete. Yet, not everyone who travels beyond the physical boundaries of the Marsh Farm is satisfied. For example, Uncle Tom's globe-trotting and Ursula's excursions into "the man's world" do not result in contentment. Then, too, after her trip to the continent, Ursula feels that she must explore what is unknown, for the old world has been swept away and she has not found a new one. Life with the Brangwens is far from bad, so Ursula is faced with a question: Should she experience the agony of going beyond herself and the life of the farm, or should she settle for the advantages of a conventional life?

There is no simple answer to this question. Ideally, Ursula would have Alfred's surety and would not have to suffer as she struggles to find new life. As she enters her twenties, however, she feels incomplete and empty. Thus, if she wants to become a stable, vital person, she must go beyond her sometimes cozy, often frustrating existence at home.

Unfortunately, there are two ways of going beyond, and Ursula chooses the wrong way first. She travels outside the farm and Cossethay, explores the physical world, and is repeatedly disillusioned. Later, however, after she and Anton go their separate ways for the second time, she goes beyond what is known and visible to what is unknown and invisible. Doing so is painful, for she discovers that only she can be responsible for the development of her inner life, or soul. But she has no choice; she has to struggle into being.

At the beginning of *The Rainbow* one of the Brangwen women anticipates Ursula by looking out "towards the activity of man in the world at large" (9). She focuses on dominant men from an unfamiliar world, just as Ursula focuses on Skrebensky, who comes to her from the strange world of the military. Like Ursula, this early Brangwen does not find it easy to turn her back on her own world. Emphasizing this, Lawrence uses the word "strained" repeatedly in the opening pages of the novel. Looking beyond, the woman "strained" to hear the sounds of "the world speaking" (8), he says. Later, referring to this person as "the woman," he tells us that "she strained her eyes to see what man had done in fighting outwards to knowledge, she strained to hear how he uttered himself in his conquest" (9). She is not part of the world of fighting, knowledge, and dominant men, however, so she begins to live vicariously. Like the women of the village, she lives "her own fulfillment" (11) through Mrs. Hardy, who has travelled.

Living vicariously, "the woman" and other women of this period can idealize a world they have not experienced: "The lady of the Hall was the living dream of their lives, her life was the epic that inspired their lives." Thrilled by Mrs. Hardy's great house, servants, and beautiful clothes, they manage to include even her "scandalous brother" and her "husband who drank" in their fantasy. They gossip about these two men and regard the vicar and Lord William as "wonderful" because they have "the power of thought and comprehension." Even the "Brangwen wife of the Marsh" aspires "towards the further life of the finer woman" (11). But, as a group, the women are "much fonder of Tom" (11), settle for him or a man like him, and remain somewhat discontented.

Discontentment is what motivates the women to look beyond their lives "in the house," but they would not aspire to social success if they knew nothing about fashionable life. Once they have heard about "the far-off world of cities and government," they feel a lack of "something" (9). Like Ursula, they cannot put into words what that something is, so they assume it is what they know about but do not have. Thus, one Brangwen woman who is ambitious for her children compares them to the curate's children. She decides that the curate's offspring are dominant "from the start" because they are educated, so she wants "education, this higher form of being" (10) for her own children. She also wants them to have what education leads to: achievement, freedom to move about, and social status.

Since Ursula is influenced by the past, she is influenced by the values of this woman and her contemporaries. Thus, in the middle of the novel, she wants what other women want at the beginning: to get out of the house, to be educated, to travel, and to know men of power who inhabit "worlds beyond" and are associated with "magic." Like her grandmother's contemporaries, she is bored and as a cure wants something "more" from the social world. She has one advantage over those women and even over Anna: her mother. She travels beyond her home, experiences the visible world, and discovers that it is not what she wants.

As time passes in the novel, the men begin to resemble the women. Discontented, they too begin to seek success and status in the social world. Thus Tom becomes a gentleman, Will becomes a teacher of art, and Uncle Tom becomes a businessman. And, like the women, they ignore their inner lives. In doing so, they fail to discover answers to the important questions raised very early in the novel: "But why should a knowledge of far-off countries make a man's life a different thing, finer, bigger? And why is a man more than the beast and the cattle that serve him?" (11). Living in the visible world of objects and bodies, the men, like the women, do not know the answers.

Ursula begins to surpass her ancestors when she learns about the soul and the limitations of the physical world. Going beyond her parents, she not only travels but also goes beyond her social self. As a result, she discovers what she is like inside, in the dark unconscious; she struggles into being, and finds new life.

To understand the nature and significance of Ursula's struggle, it is necessary to begin with Lydia and Tom, for they are the first Brangwens to struggle as a result of the rift that began to develop at the time that Alfred married the woman from Heanor. At the same time, it is important to keep Alfred and the woman from Heanor in mind, for they have the surety that Ursula wants so badly.

Chapter 6

Tom and Lydia:
The "Invisible Connexion"

Alfred Brangwen and the woman from Heanor have a good relationship. Although she often mortifies him, she is the object of his love and affection. At the same time, he feels "like a lord of creation" (13) and does whatever he feels like doing. As Lawrence's brief description of them suggests, they have strength and are fulfilled. But they are not model individuals whom others should try to imitate; they are inimitable because they are unique. Nevertheless, they are reminders that people can be confident and vitally connected to one another; they have surety.

One generation later, Tom also has surety and is brimming with life, although he has to struggle to establish a relationship with a woman and to express the life that is within him. Trapped in a changing community and influenced by the desecration of the land, he lives among people who mistakenly turn to the visible, material world for satisfaction. In this world people have begun to accept what Lord Chatterley takes for granted in *Lady Chatterley's Lover,* namely, that nothing is real except what the eye can see and the mind can know, and even Tom Brangwen is somewhat affected by this belief. Influenced by his contemporaries, he cannot accept that an invisible connection with another person is either possible or valuable, so he must learn from his experiences.

His most important experience is a relationship with Lydia Lensky, a Polish woman. To attain and then maintain a relationship with her, Tom must struggle, but not as fiercely as Ursula does when, two generations later, she tries to establish a relationship with Skrebensky. As a Brangwen who spends many hours a day in the open fields, Tom is more compatible with his world than Ursula is with hers. Then, too, he has much more confidence intrinsically. As a very young man, he has the surety that she needs to develop slowly as she experiences the material world. Nevertheless, Tom must exert himself if he wants to connect with Lydia and, in doing so, feel complete.

To be complete Tom must resist the values of his contemporaries, and at the same time he must do battle with himself, for he resists a connection even as he craves it. Lydia has a similar difficulty, so the Tom-Lydia relationship is characterized by ebb and flow for a long time. At one point she is "unfolded" and ready to receive Tom, but, after a few days, she closes and becomes impervious to him. Then she opens "towards him, to flow towards him again" (56), but, almost at once, she feels like a stranger again. Similarly, he is alternately attracted to and repelled by Lydia. At one moment he feels keenly her separate and remote nature. Then, suddenly, there is a "connexion between them again" (62) and, just as suddenly, he once more regards her as cold and remote. Clearly, the relationship does not flow smoothly at all times. Fearing what they want so badly, both Tom and Lydia disrupt the flow by vacillating.

This does not mean that they lack confidence. Instead, they perceive and respond to the threats that are a real part of any relationship. When they express their feelings, they become vulnerable and are hurt. When they acquiesce to the other person's needs, they may be dominated. When they cease to exert their wills, they feel obliterated. Then, too, because their relationship is vital, they express new life as they touch, and newness is a threat. Describing Lydia's response to a "new birth" in herself and "new life" in Tom, Lawrence writes: "A shiver, a sickness of new birth passed over her, the flame leaped up him, under his skin. She wanted it, this new life from him, with him, yet she must defend herself against it, for it was a destruction" (40). Clearly, Lydia fears what she craves.

Tom also fears what he craves: a "robust" relationship with Lydia; at the same time, he feels "obliterated" when he kisses her. And when she leans forward and kisses him, he regards her mouth as "ugly-beautiful," that is, he finds it both attractive and repellant. When he holds her in his arms, he experiences the "blenched agony" of breaking "away from himself" (46), so the relationship is threatened. Fortunately, Tom has confidence, courage, and a strong desire to have a connection with Lydia, so he is able to come to grips with feelings that originate within himself. Accordingly, he survives the destructive aspects of their relationship and discovers, through experience, "a new life" that makes him feel complete and is beyond conception, that is, cannot be known in the mind.

He must also cope with external threats to his well-being: the dissolving community and the ravaged countryside; both are disconcerting, both affect the individual, and both are unavoidable. Inevitably, the materialism of the community will influence Tom, and the smoke, odors, and sounds from the pit will afflict his senses. Thus, he cannot avoid what influences his contemporaries and, if he is affected, his relationship with Lydia will be affected too.

Underscoring that no one can avoid the community's influence, Lawrence stresses Tom's close connection with other people at the beginning of *The Rainbow*. He does this by presenting Tom as an individual who is also a Brangwen, and emphasizes that Brangwens are part of a larger group. Drawing attention to this in part 1 of chapter 1 (7–11), he mentions Tom Brangwen by name but refers to the other Brangwens generically. They are the Brangwens, the men, the women, they, she, the woman, Brangwen, the mother, and the Brangwen wife of the Marsh. At times it is not easy to determine which Brangwen Lawrence has in mind. Then, too, he allows the values of the Brangwen women to merge with the values of the village women. Both groups live vicariously through Mrs. Hardy and the other "fine" women and men who prosper in the material world. Lawrence calls the lives of the Brangwens, the women of the village, and the people living at Shelly Hall a "poem." In doing so, he indicates that the separate and related groups and individuals who live near the Marsh Farm are a cohesive community.

Lawrence reinforces the sense of community in part 2 of chapter 1.

Having mentioned Tom by name twice in part 1, he begins part 2 with several references to "the Brangwens," a group of people living in the meadows. Soon, however, individuals emerge from that group. Lawrence mentions Alfred Senior first and then, in rapid succession, his children. Using this means of introducing the Brangwens to his readers, he can stress that they are individuals who grow out of a community that has group values.

At the same time, this cohesive community is beginning to dissolve, and the women are dissatisfied. No longer rooted in their traditional roles, in relationship to their husbands who still have traditional roles, the women have found a center of existence outside the farmhouse, the farm, and the meadow. Certainly, they can "get along, whatever their lot," but they need "the wonder of the beyond" (11) to do so. Besides, the land surrounding the farm has also changed; it is still enclosed and shut off from the pits, but it is no longer isolated. Instead, the whistles and the sounds of engines leap across space and cause the Brangwens to be distracted from the land beneath their feet. Distracted, they feel less rooted in the soil, and the rootedness of their existence is disturbed.

It is not possible to say exactly when the disturbance began. Mudrick says that "the coming of the colliery . . . , bringing canal and railway through the Brangwen land," occurred "years before" Tom met Lydia.[1] But, like the opening words of part 2 of chapter 1 ("About 1840"), "years before" is inexact. Much of the opening section is inexact although exactness characterizes the remainder of the novel. Even individual words such as "ash," "root," "beyond," "unknown," and "surety" are used so carefully that any thoughtful reader must wonder why Lawrence is not equally precise at the beginning of The Rainbow.

There is an explanation: Lawrence wants to make a statement about the manner in which change affects different people. In particular, he wants to establish that people are affected by their environment (including other people), but that it does not affect them the way a physical force affects an inanimate object. The environment alone never compels a person to respond in one way only. Thus, in chapter 1 of The Rainbow, Lawrence emphasizes that the invasion of the meadows by technology has a profound influence on the lives of the characters eventually; however, it is not possible to say exactly when that influence begins. At the same time, not everyone is affected in the same way. Instead, what a person is, intrinsically, combines with the environment to produce unique and unpredictable changes within that person.

To underscore this point, Lawrence introduces the Brangwens to his readers at a time much later than 1840, that is, long after machines have begun to destroy the land. For some unspecified period of time the machines have influenced the characters. Connected to the outside world by ugly sights and sounds, they know that there is an existence beyond the Marsh Farm, so they strain to break free from their setting. They are also discontented; their discontentment, however, is not inevitable. If it were, all of them would be affected in the same way and at the same time, but they are not. To begin with, the women become discontented long before the men do. Then, too, Tom is far less affected than his brothers. Emphasizing this in a progress report on the three Brangwen brothers, Lawrence says that Frank has developed a "grievance against the world" and Alfred Junior has become contemptuous, but Tom is "very fresh and alert, with zest for every moment of life" (18–19). Clearly, in *The Rainbow* the community and the land affect different people differently. While some are diminished, at least one character continues to thrive as a person.

There are several reasons that characters respond differently to their situation. To begin with, different people reacting to the same set of circumstances make conscious choices. They cannot be indifferent or unaffected, and they cannot make any choice they want. As Lawrence says, however, they can choose from among their many desires. Then, too, different combinations of circumstances affect each individual at any one time. For example, the invasion of the land has an effect on Tom and his brothers, but other circumstances act only on Tom. Specifically, he is his mother's favorite and becomes manager of the Marsh Farm at a very early age. As a result, he is more emotionally developed than his brothers, learns responsibility, and derives vitality (or at least stability) from the land he works on many hours a day. And, finally, no matter how much he resembles other Brangwens, he is intrinsically different. He is unique. Consequently, the effect on him of external things—the land, the community, his mother and other individuals—is both unique and unpredictable.

Because he is unique and living in a unique place at a specific time, Tom cannot hope for typical satisfaction (or fulfillment). If he wants satisfaction, he must assume responsibility for his own life, and in doing so he cannot follow a prescribed pattern of behavior. After all, what worked for others in the past will not work for him in his changing world. Thus he has no choice; living in a world that is not in every way continuous with his father's world, he must be guided by his own experiences. Slowly and painfully he must develop his own religion, or beliefs. As part of this evolving process, he must be guided by the effect of his experiences on his invisible inner life or, as Lawrence says, on his soul. If he values inner experience at least as much as he values the material world that so many of his contemporaries value exclusively, he will discover that "the supreme triumph is to be most vividly, most perfectly alive."[2] First, however, he must engage in the difficult struggle into being.

Tom's struggle into being begins long before he meets Lydia. As with everything else that affects the development of people in *The Rainbow*, however, it is not possible to say exactly when the struggle begins. Certainly Tom's frustrating experiences in school are a part of that struggle; so are his reactions to his parents' deaths. And, beyond a doubt, his first sexual experience is crucial. It is useful to study Tom's experience with illicit sex carefully; it reveals a great deal about his unwillingness to settle for the visible world only.

When Tom is nineteen, he visits a prostitute. He is drunk at the time and is tormented "with sex desires" (20). He also idealizes women. For him the woman is "the symbol for that further life which comprised religion and love and morality." Then, too, he is close to the females in his family: at nineteen he is still "like a plant rooted in his mother and sister" (19). When he realizes that he has lain with a prostitute, he is shocked. For the first time he feels mistrust, and he begins to think about himself and his connection with women.

Outwardly, he remains unchanged. A casual observer would notice "his blue eyes just as clear and honest as ever, his face just as fresh, his appetite just as keen" (20). But inwardly, in his soul, he is less confident, less buoyant, and more disillusioned. Like Ursula, he experiences "a first taste of ash" as a result of experiencing sex that is strictly physical. And, again like Ursula, he fears that all his sexual relations will be "this nothingness" (19). So he withdraws from society and avoids women, "but the business of love was, at the bottom of his soul, the most serious and terrifying of all to him" (20). After a while, he recovers somewhat, but when his mother dies, he responds to stress the way some other Brangwens do—he drinks a great deal. He also has a brief fling with the mistress of a foreigner, wants to get married, wants "something" that he cannot name, wants to travel, and resents "the cold material of his customary life" (26).

Much later in the novel, Ursula's behavior is reminiscent of Tom's. When her relationship with Skrebensky is failing, she, too, tastes the ash of disillusion in her mouth, considers marriage, wants "something" that she cannot name, reacts negatively to the world of material objects, and wants to travel. As she is a Brangwen, she behaves like one, but she is not a carbon copy of Tom by any means; both characters are unique in their own way.

Tom is unique when it comes to expressing his anger. Like Ursula, he is capable of great hostility. When she destroys Skrebensky with her kisses and annihilates him psychologically, Ursula denies that she has been hostile. She even convinces herself that she is good and loving and, outwardly, continues to behave as if she is warm and ordinary. By doing so, she soothes her conscience, but, inwardly, she pays a price: "her soul was empty and finished" (323). In contrast, Tom grows "into a raging fury against" Lydia and denies nothing. Acknowledging that he is afraid of destroying the relationship by becoming too angry, he decides, consciously, to make "no retaliation on her" (62). As a result, he can preserve his connection with Lydia and, unlike Ursula, does not have to engage in a long, self-destructive battle to make the unconscious conscious. Because his conscious thoughts do not conflict with his feelings to the extent that Ursula's do, he has surety.

He needs surety to make a relationship with Lydia viable. She is, after all, an exceptionally strong and vital woman who might overwhelm a weaker man. Then, too, Lawrence emphasizes what he calls Lydia's otherness, that is, the quality that keeps her intrinsically separate and apart from him. She is foreign (part Polish and part German), has had a child (Anna) by another man, wears that man's wedding ring, is six years older than Tom, and has manners that seem strange to him. Even more important, she is different from him emotionally and temperamentally. Nevertheless, when he sees her for the first time, he says, involuntarily, "That's her." Convinced that they have exchanged recognition, he intends to marry her (29).

In Lawrence's fiction marriage does not resolve differences and conflicts. Married or unmarried, strong men and women must battle one another before they can establish a relationship. Intent on preserving their individuality, they exert their will initially and, ultimately, may try to dominate one another. But according to Lawrence, there is no relationship when one person dominates. Then, too, if both the man and the woman refuse to give in, that is, refuse to relinquish their will, they experience only conflict and cannot express the life that is within them.

Both Tom and Lydia give in eventually. As a result, they pass "through the doorway into the further space" (95) together. "She was the doorway to him, he to her" (96), Lawrence says. First, however, each must address the threat that the other seems to embody and, at times, actually is. Each must accept that the other is other than oneself and cannot be known in the mind. Also, each must adapt to the other's anger and his own. When Tom becomes hostile or Lydia turns on him "like a tiger" (63), both must accept that aggression is a part of human nature. Having done so, both must be willing to engage in the struggle that leads to "the doorway into the further space."

For Tom, the struggle with Lydia begins as soon as he feels they have exchanged recognition. Immediately he has self-doubts and because of his encounter with the prostitute he fears disillusionment. The "doubt was like a sense of infinite space, a nothingness, annihilating" (29–30), but he does not succumb to negativism; instead, encouraged by the exchange of recognition, he keeps "within his breast the will to surety" (30). As a result, he feels an inner connection.

This inner connection is essential to the success of the Tom-Lydia relationship: If either had relied on the visible world, on what the eye can see and the mind can know, no relationship would have been possible in the long run. After all, Lydia is formally educated, was married to a brilliant doctor, and has travelled. She is sophisticated. In contrast, Tom had difficulty with formal education, has never left his birthplace, and is coarse. But each has inner strength and relies on it when the other person seems to be a threat. For example, there are times when Tom is afraid of Lydia. Aware of how separate and remote she is, he defends himself against fear by becoming hostile, but he is wise enough to know that reacting against her personally, that is, against her person, will solve nothing. Fortunately, "he had made some invisible connexion with the strange woman" (39), and he relies on this. As a result, "All these things were only words to him, the fact of her superior birth, the fact that her husband had been a brilliant doctor, the fact that he himself was her inferior in almost every way of distinction. There was an inner reality, a logic of the soul, which connected her with him" (41).

Having surety, Tom can accept the inner reality as greater than the reality of the visible world. Accordingly, he can accept impersonal love as superior to personal love. Personal love changes as the other person changes outwardly (for example, grows older). In contrast, impersonal love is inviolable, according to Lawrence. Experienced deep within the individual as an invisible connection with another individual, it is both true and real. Thus Tom gradually comes to know Lydia "even without seeing her" (40). In their relationship the invisible soul is important.

The body is also important in their relationship. Once the invisible connection is made, bodily contact is especially satisfying. Although Tom and Lydia meet as strangers in the vicar's kitchen and "must for ever be such strangers," when they touch they experience "Such intimacy of embrace, and such utter foreignness of contact" (49) that the whole world seems to be charged with brilliant energy. Yet they do not know each other mentally, and the other person remains the unknown.

Experiencing the unknown and acknowledging its value, Tom can control his fear of Lydia, but he faces other problems. He feels tension, anticipates rejection, and is often angry. He could have ended the relationship and returned to his drinking, his isolation, and his routine existence. He could have played it safe. But he chooses another route because he discovers, through experience, that his desire to have a relationship with Lydia is stronger than his fear of one. This discovery comes when "during the long February nights with the ewes in labour . . . , he knew he did not belong to himself." As a man who has surety, he could stand alone and still survive, but he would be "only fragmentary, something incomplete and subject." So, although it is "a hard experience," he admits that "without her he was nothing" (40–41).

Some readers consider Tom's refusal to stand alone evidence of his weakness. In doing so, they support the ideal that people should be willing to stand alone on principle, regardless of the consequences. Lawrence eschews ideals and presents instead the inner condition of people who remain independent; they are fragments and must remain unsatisfied. Whether or not they will admit it, people need one another for fulfillment. The strongest males and females in Lawrence's fiction accept mature dependence on a person of the opposite sex. Strong people are able to give in, acquiesce, or submit themselves to the other person without feeling slavish or degraded. Tom, for example, acknowledges that he needs Lydia, but he does not feel diminished. Following obliteration in her arms, "he had a completeness and an inviolable power" (47). He is unperturbed by a reminder that she had another life before she met him and is still separate from him. Having made invisible contact with a woman he does not know mentally, he responds casually even when she is indifferent to him later. In contrast to Will, who cannot acquiesce to Anna during his honeymoon, Tom is strong enough to acquiesce to the innate human need for a relationship.

Having the strength to acquiesce does not guarantee the success of a relationship; the other person must also acquiesce. Lydia must meet Tom as stranger to stranger and yet be receptive. At the same time, she must come to him as an individual. Emphasizing this, Lawrence focuses on Tom first, and then on Lydia. He says very little about Lydia's inner life until page forty. Then, at the beginning of chapter 2 he shifts the emphasis to her. "She was the daughter of a Polish landowner," he says (50), and then proceeds to fill in her background, thus stressing her individuality without making her personal. Details about her life in Poland make her seem more remote than ever. Connected to Tom, she nevertheless experiences the world as a separate individual.

Tom and Lydia: The "Invisible Connexion"

Existing separately, she remains unknown to Tom. Although he finds this painful, he does not idealize her, that is, he does not convert her into his idea of what a woman should be so that he can know her mentally and thus have some control in the relationship. Instead, he reveres the unknown even as he fears it. As a result, he makes a relationship possible, but Lydia deserves much of the credit for the success of that relationship. Like Tom, she struggles when she encounters a person of the opposite sex. At times she even takes the initiative to keep the relationship alive. First, however, she needs to overcome the experience of her devastating first marriage.

As a young woman, Lydia married a man "full of words" and consented to be his servant. She went through the motions of being a "good" wife and even nursed her husband as he was dying; however, when he was dead, she felt neither loss nor grief, but she remains nearly devastated by her bitter experience of marriage. Years later, she still shrinks from life and remains "blotted safely away from living" (53). In time, however, she returns to life, demanding that it be what it had been when she was young, but she is unable to recover her youth. Alone and independent, she is only a fragment or, as Lawrence says, she is "like a flower that comes above-ground to find a great stone lying above it" (55). Like Tom, she is helpless and needs someone.

Although Tom is nearly inarticulate and is Lydia's social inferior, he is the man Lydia needs because he affects her so strongly physically. When he walks by, she trembles in her body and feels that he has actually brushed her. Nevertheless, even as she is about to waken physically, she resists. Still affected by her first marriage, she lapses "into the old unconsciousness, indifference, and there was a will in her to save herself from living any more" (55). Then, too, because contact with Tom earlier startled her "out of herself" (44), she is afraid. So, like her lover, she has to overcome fears that originate within her.

To prevail against her fear she must learn from her experiences; in particular, she must learn that she cannot control life by exerting her will. Instead, she must relax and become "like a flower unsheathed in the sun," for then she can "feel her blood running" (55). Before she is capable of letting go, she is locked in conflict. Fearing what she wants so much, she is caught between living and not living. At the relatively superficial level of impulse, she is "strong against" Tom, but at the deep level of instinct, she wants to "relinquish herself to him" (55).

After a while instinct wins out over impulse. Tired of being the unrooted flower lying above the ground, and attracted to Tom's "rooted safety . . . and the life in him" (55), she lets herself go, suspends her will, and feels herself "opening, unfolding, asking, as a flower opens in full request under the sun" (56). When Tom balks, she becomes confused and finds it "cruel . . . to be opened and offered to him" (57), but soon she decides there is nothing to balk at, so they are married.

Their commitment to marriage is part of their struggle to come together. Eschewing ideals, they accept the whole of marriage: the wonderful moments and the passion, but also the fears, frustrations, and hostilities that surface when they try to "come through." Tom's acceptance of Lydia is a reflection of this total acceptance, which develops gradually.

At first, Tom cannot tolerate Lydia's mouth because it is "ugly-beautiful" rather than simply beautiful. He notices her "ugly wide mouth" even on their wedding day. And, later, he finds ugliness in her character: She is willful and hostile, regards the peasants in Poland as cattle, and finds it amusing, even in retrospect, that naked girls were paraded through a village in a truck. Nevertheless, he wants "to mingle with her, losing himself to find her, to find himself in her" (95). Knowing about Poland and Paul Lensky, "he understood no more of this in her," but he does know her meaning "without understanding" (96), so he accepts her as she is, in her entirety, and accepts marriage with her.

Their marriage, like their courtship, does not always flow smoothly. Occasionally, they exclude each other from their lives. For example, when Tom becomes frustrated, he stays away from home and Lydia withdraws into herself. They become alienated from one another. "She did not feel she had married him," and he feels that a "gap, a space opened before him" (93). Perceiving correctly that contact with his brother's mistress has made Tom despise himself, Lydia does what she does typically: she takes the initiative and challenges Tom. The resulting encounter is great and rewarding.

Tom and Lydia: The "Invisible Connexion"

At the beginning of the encounter, Lydia remarks, "To you I am nothing—it is like cattle" (94). Saying this, she brings to mind a question raised at the beginning of the novel: "And why is a man more than the beast and the cattle that serve him?" (11). So, briefly, Tom (and readers of the novel) must consider that people are, indeed, only cattle. They may be like cows, bodies without souls; and the "invisible connexion" that Tom believes he has with Lydia may be only an illusion.

Fortunately, Lydia does not let the challenge go unheeded. "Come here," she says to Tom, and he acquiesces, although doing so requires "an almost deathly effort of volition." To him, she is still the "awful unknown," but she is undaunted. Committing herself, she puts her arms around him and says, "My love!" (94). Still frightened, he nevertheless is affected by the emotional contact that she initiates and, as a result, experiences her as transfigured, wonderful, and beyond him. At this point, he is vulnerable and she could destroy him as Ursula destroys Skrebensky, but Lydia does not want a victory. Instead, she wants Tom's active participation. Nevertheless, he is unable "to give himself to her actively" for a while; he is too frightened. "Then gradually, the tension, the withholding relaxed in him, and he began to flow towards her" (95).

As a result of their commitment, both Lydia and Tom have their reward: "baptism to another life" and "complete confirmation" (95). Together they experience what Lawrence calls "the transfiguration, the glorification, the admission" (96). The invisible, nonmental, and impersonal bond between them is strengthened.

Lawrence emphasizes the strength and the importance of that bond in several ways. To begin with, he describes their sexual coming together by using words that have religious connotations: baptism, another life, transfiguration, and glorification. He indicates that the husband-wife relationship is the most important one for Tom and Lydia; it replaces the God-man relationship. Then, too, he stresses the couple's separateness and relatedness simultaneously. They do not think about each other consciously after their great encounter; instead, they go their separate ways. When they touch, however, they know each other instantly. And, finally, he emphasizes Tom and Lydia's belief in marriage. Experiencing marriage as "an inexhaustible exploration" rather than a cul-de-sac, Lydia becomes "active and always pleased, intent" (102), and Tom becomes an outspoken advocate of marriage. At Anna's wedding, he makes a humorous but serious defense of marriage, asserting that "a married couple makes one Angel" (138).

To be sure, not everyone in *The Rainbow* shares Tom and Lydia's view of marriage. In the midst of Tom's wedding speech, other wedding guests jeer him, indicating that their experience with marriage has been different from his. Then, too, both Tom and Lydia have lives that are not entirely satisfying. She limits herself by making her husband and her children "her horizon" (102); he acknowledges that he has known satisfaction with Lydia, but claims that "he was *not* satisfied" (129). His interest in social success, his inability to overcome his fear of the unknown, and his great difficulty in giving up Anna to Will are all evidence that his life is not perfect. He lives a bit too much in terms of outward things.

Nevertheless, the bond between Tom and Lydia is strong. It nourishes their bodies and their souls and makes physical satisfaction, and even delight, possible. Then, too, once the bond is established, the two exist in equilibrium; there is no winner or loser, as there is with Anna and Will. At times, Tom does have the urge to control Lydia. Generally, however, there is give and take. As Lawrence says, "When she called, he answered, when he asked, her response came at once, or at length" (96). So, despite some imperfections, their marriage is satisfying.

It is satisfying because both the husband and the wife have surety. Inwardly vital and confident, they are not overwhelmed by what is external to themselves, including other people. They suffer temporary setbacks, but ultimately they work through their problems and accept life in its entirety. Overcoming the desire to abstract from life whatever pleases and to ignore the rest, they accept what Blake would call contraries: love and aggression, body and soul, what is known and what can only be experienced. As a result, they do not live exclusively for social status, physical love, and wealth.

This does not mean that the visible world is inconsequential; it affects every generation of Brangwens and, in fact, becomes increasingly important to Tom as he grows older. But neither he nor Lydia is limited to (or by) the material world. Inevitably, they experience the material world first, but they pass beyond it to what is invisible and unknown. At one point Tom experiences something well beyond himself: the infinite, unchanging world.

When Lydia is in labor, she is as different from Tom and as remote as she will ever be. They respond to one another, but their response is not personal. Tom is keenly aware that she is "other than himself," and Lydia knows him not as himself but as "the man," so she gives him "an impersonal look, in the extreme hour, female to male." But from experience Tom knows the value of the impersonal response, so, tortured and at peace, he leaves the house, feels "the darkness striking unseen and steadily upon him," and is overcome, finally, by the "unseen threshing of the night." When he returns to the house, he has no doubts: "There was the infinite world, eternal, unchanging, as well as the world of life" (81).

Chapter 7

Anna and Tom: "Infinite Sensual Violence"

Just before Anna and Will are married, Tom takes a cottage for them at Cossethay. The place has everything: a large kitchen, cupboards, a garden, and a row of yew trees along one side. In addition, Tom buys "handy little things" for Anna: cooking pans, a fashionable lamp, and a machine for grinding food (131). The greatest gift is a mangle, the latest device for wringing clothes. Tom enjoys purchasing it, Tilly exclaims that this "latest contraption" will save people a lot of work, and Anna turns the handle "with great gusto of possession" (132), so everyone is happy, even Will. After all, the new house containing the gadgets is situated alongside his beloved church.

Responding to the house and the gadgets, Anna, Tom, Tilly, and Will are in character, and their behavior is ordinary. At the same time, their responses are significant in that they reveal something about their characters. This is especially true of Tom. Having become wealthier without discovering a purpose to existence beyond his immediate family, he values visible objects more than he once did: "He was never happy unless he was buying something" (131). Clearly, he has begun to value money for its own sake.

Neither he nor Lydia was indifferent to security a generation earlier.

Anna and Tom: "Infinite Sensual Violence"

Meeting in the vicar's kitchen, they discussed property briefly. "It is your own place, the house, the farm—?" she asked, but when he responded simply, "Yes" (37), they dropped the subject. Interested in security, neither Tom nor Lydia expressed any interest in luxuries.

By the time Anna and Will marry, Tom has found a use for luxuries. They distract him, and he needs distraction. Beyond a doubt, he has known both pleasure and satisfaction with Lydia, but something is missing from his life. Furthermore, because he is inarticulate, he cannot say what that something is, but it is obvious to readers that he, like Will, does not have a "real purposive self" (238). Consequently, Tom makes spending money his purpose, but in doing so he does not gain the satisfaction he craves. Yet for moments at a time he is happy, so he continues to spend. Neither community values nor his own experience has taught him to respond differently.

Although Tom may have become more materialistic, he still has surety and he still has Lydia. After all, in Lawrence's fiction, surety does not guarantee total satisfaction; nevertheless, it makes satisfaction possible between two people even when they are radically different from one another. Commenting on this, Marvin Mudrick writes, "The temperamental differences between Lydia and Tom were unbridgeable, and of no significance to Lydia"[1]; nor do the differences matter to Tom. Having surety, he can connect invisibly with a socially superior woman. To be sure, if Tom had not met Lydia, he might never have known satisfaction with a woman. Conversely, although he has surety, he remains dissatisfied in some respects simply because in the modern world he cannot find an activity that will give purpose to his life.

A generation later Anna and Will do not have either Lydia's or Tom's surety and thus they don't learn of the possibility of satisfaction in marriage. Eventually Anna is aware of the lack in herself. "She was uneasy," Lawrence says, presenting Anna's point of view. "The surety, the surety, the inner surety, the confidence in the abidingness of love: that was what she wanted. And that she did not get" (167). Nor is she likely to "get" it since she refuses to assume responsibility for developing her own inner life. Instead, she blames others, especially Will, for her "lack of stability." By doing so she foregoes the opportunity to grow and to develop inner confidence. Because Will, too, lacks surety, she could not have an "invisible connexion" with him unless he also assumed responsibility for growing as an individual. But he does not and perhaps cannot, so neither he nor she even begins that struggle into being that makes it possible for couples to experience sexual satisfaction in addition to sexual pleasure.

Compared to the Tom-Lydia struggle, Will and Anna's is a war. But they do not struggle to make the unconscious conscious, that is, they do not acknowledge and then come to grips with fears and feelings that exist deep within them. In particular, they do not work through their anger and hostility; instead, they fight "an unknown battle, unconsciously," a battle that Lawrence describes as deep, fierce, and unnamed (168). After a while, even their love-making is a battle: they are like two hawks, or two enemies retaliating (163). Because they lack surety, they react as if their very lives are at stake. Eventually, they fight so fiercely that there can be no resolution, or peace, until one is the victor and the other is the vanquished.

Although Anna and Will inherit the potential to be vital and confident, to realize that potential they must seek out and live in the world of "knowledge and experience"; they must interact with people in the community. Because the community is dissolving, neither Anna nor Will feels attached to it. Then, too, even as a child, Anna was the center of her world rather than an integral part of it; and Will feels very little connection with anything concrete. When they become lovers, they reinforce one another's habit of avoiding any serious involvement with the external world.

They know that the world is out there, but they regard it as the rim, or the rind, of their existence. Thus, they try to "create a new thing by themselves" (115) when they are courting and on their honeymoon they remain inside their new house. They even lock the door and close the blinds so that they are "as remote from the world as if the two of them were buried like a seed in darkness" (145). But they do not germinate in the darkness and, because they are a single seed, neither reacts to the other as a separate entity. For a while they enjoy the illusion that they have escaped from involvement and entanglement with other people. Eventually, however, Will opens the window and discovers that the "world *was* there, after all" (147). Consequently, both he and Anna have to adopt a new strategy to avoid the world of experience.

The new strategy, both subtler and more complex than the old one, first involves making use of the other person in a new way. For a while Anna behaves as if Will is "just the bright reflex of herself," that is, before she realizes that he is "something dark, alien to herself" and even "a dark opposite to her." Lacking surety, she feels threatened by his otherness, becomes defensive, and tries to justify her defensiveness. She convinces herself that she is "a flower that has been tempted forth into blossom, and has no retreat." As the passive voice suggests, she believes that she has been acted upon and tricked into exposing herself. She even convinces herself that Will is "the unknown to which she was delivered up." In reality, however, she is trying to avoid any real, or vital, connection with people, including Will, because as Lawrence says, presenting her point of view, "She wanted to preserve herself" (169), that is, she wants to remain separate and intact. As a separate person, she can remain independent and will not have to assume responsibility for interacting with others and developing her own inner life.

Will, too, eschews responsibility for his life. This becomes obvious in Will's reaction when, suddenly, Anna decides to give a tea party. "It made him frightened and furious and miserable," Lawrence says. "He was afraid all would be lost that he had so newly come into" (151). Anna remains blithely indifferent until, finally, Will's mere presence begins to irritate her, and she turns on him "blindly and destructively." Unable to acquiesce to the situation and unable to understand Anna's intentions, Will becomes "complete in his own tense, black will. He was now unaware of her. She did not exist" (152). In brief, he behaves as Anna behaves: he isolates himself from his mate and blames her entirely for the failure of their relationship. He gains something by justifying his black mood; but at the same time, he loses a great deal. In choosing to be dependent on Anna rather than taking on his share of responsibility for himself, he makes a relationship with Anna impossible and, as a result, cannot grow.

Because Lawrence stresses Will's dependence and Anna's independence, one may misinterpret her behavior as superior to his. Lawrence does not regard independence as an absolute good; in "We Need One Another" he defines it as the desire to have nothing to do with other people.[2] Thus, Will's immature dependence on Anna is not necessarily a strength, but her denial of all dependence is a weakness. Anna regards Will as merely an adjunct to herself and feels oppressed when he is near her for any length of time. In contrast, he identifies so closely with her that he does not experience her as a separate, distinct being; consequently, when she is absent he is forlorn. And, all the while, each is a limited, undeveloped individual. As Lawrence says, they are fragments.

As fragments, both Anna and Will are dissatisfied and insecure. Because they are insecure, they experience anything they cannot control as a threat. Thus, Anna does not mind Will's presence before she realizes that he is not an extension of her. At times her greatest fear is that he will become oblivious of her and that he and she will "go hard and separate again" (169); then, suddenly, she wants nothing to do with him, seemingly for no reason, but there is a reason. As a person who conceives of her soul and her self as "one and the same" (159), she perceives any threat to her body as a threat to her entire being. So when Will seems to be dark, threatening, and separate, she fears "annihilation." Blaming him for what she experiences subjectively, she tries to isolate herself from him. When this fails, she tries to control him. Because her problem is internal, neither strategy works. She has failed to realize that she has developed one part of her self, the physical, and ignored her soul.

In contrast, Will has ignored the physical part of himself. When he is married, he does not "care about himself as a human being," nor does he "attach any vital importance to his life in the drafting office, or his life among men" (158). And, even earlier, this one-sidedness affects his relationship with Anna: "In himself, he knew her. But his outward faculties seemed suspended. He did not see her with his eyes" (130). So while his body is the only reality to Anna, hers is virtually nonexistent to him. Yet he experiences her as a portion of himself. As a result, when she is not present physically, he feels that something within himself is missing. Being a soulful person who cannot connect with himself physically, he feels incomplete, like a fragment.

Conventional wisdom prescribes that opposites attract and, for a while, this seems to apply to Anna and Will. "For three days they had been immune in a perfect love" (153), Lawrence says, but then the outside world intrudes and makes them conscious of their separateness and their differences. Lacking inner strength, each seeks to control everything external, including other people. This need for control is so strong that it arouses hostility when it is frustrated. For Will, who wants to be good, simply being aware of his hostility is a problem. For Anna, the problem is somewhat different. She feels herself opening up, like a flower, and, on one occasion she even feels "transported to another world," that is, she loses control over her own deep feelings. Hating and resisting this loss of control, she checks and channels her feelings by directing her "dark, violent hatred" (160) at something specific: Will.

After making him the object of her hatred, Anna tries to dispose of Will by blocking him out of her life. When that fails, she tries to dominate him. But he does not give in at once, so the battle between them begins. In the chapter called "Anna Victrix" she wins that battle. As soon as she knows she has won, however, "an ashy desolation came over her" (172). Clearly, victory implies loss even for the victor.

Nevertheless, Anna and Will do experience delight and "a passion of voluptuousness" (236) eventually. What they experience is solely physical; it includes no love or tenderness and leaves out the soul. Lawrence calls it "infinite sensual violence" and "a sensuality violent and extreme as death" (237). But their experience radically changes Anna and Will's inner lives and, in addition, frees Will so that he develops "a real purposive self" (238). But their relationship is not satisfying. It is drastically different from the Tom-Lydia relationship, as a closer reading reveals.

Early in *The Rainbow,* Lawrence introduces Tom first and then Lydia. In doing so, he emphasizes their separateness. He does the same with Anna and Will. After introducing Anna, he devotes a great deal of time to describing her childhood, revealing what happens to her and what she is like at different stages of her life. For example, when she is nine, she goes to school at Cossethay; at seventeen she is touchy, spirited, and moody. Nothing in her background has prepared her for living in equilibrium with another person: She has learned to expect deference and to be contemptuous of responsibility. She also expects attention. As Lawrence says, "She was too much the centre of her own universe, too little aware of anything outside" (98).

Her relationship with Tom reinforces her egocentricity. He makes her his favorite and forms a "centre of love" (83) in her. Then, too, because Lydia devotes so much attention to Tom Junior, Anna becomes independent of her mother, loves "from her own centre," (84) and chooses to love Tom, who makes too much fuss over her. Tom secretly wants to make her a lady just as his mother wanted to make him a gentleman. As a result, Anna soon has an ideal: "a free, proud lady absolved from the petty ties, existing beyond petty considerations" (102). At sixteen, she actively pursues this ideal and becomes "a lofty demoiselle" (103).

For a while, behaving like a lofty lady causes no problems because she and Tom live an isolated existence (as she and Will do later). But when she has to go out into the world where people do not defer to her, immediately there are problems. She hates anyone who has authority over her, feels she is usually at fault, and distrusts not only the outside world but herself. When she mixes with people, she feels dominated and degraded, so she begins to think about getting away.

At first, she simply wants to get away from home; however, because life with the Brangwens has been "rich," everything in the outside world seems thin, so she returns home and tries to talk to her father, who refuses to discuss anything. Reacting as if he has snubbed her, she feels hurt and even believes that Tom has turned against her.

When she meets Will she feels that "In him she had escaped. In him the bounds of her experience were transgressed: he was the hole in the wall, beyond which the sunshine blazed on an outside world" (114). At least this is what she believes, but, in reality, she has not escaped. In regarding Will as the whole world she also sees him as a "reflex of herself," that is, she creates the illusion that the whole world is an adjunct to herself. Blinded by her love for Will, she can foster this illusion easily and, in doing so, maintain her position as the center of her universe. At times, however, she is aware that Will, and therefore the outside world, is separate and distinct, and this creates a conflict in her. For example, when she tells Will that she loves him, she acknowledges his separateness and feels pain. "It sounded as if it were tearing her" (118).

Using Will to escape from entanglement with the world is a mistake, but it works for a while. After all, because she hates to be dominated and expects to be fussed over, Anna has reasons for liking Will. He is passive, well-mannered, and deferential, and he follows her like a shadow. He also speaks well, like Anna's natural father (Paul Lensky). Then, too, during courtship he seldom touches or kisses her, so they can be "separate, single" (121). In the long run, however, they cannot remain separate, as is stressed in several ways in the beautiful scene in which they gather sheaves in the moonlight. Whereas he evokes their separateness when the gathering of sheaves begins, Lawrence also describes the setting and atmosphere in sexual terms. The shocks are "erect," and the rest of the field is "open and prostrate." Frightened, Anna wants to remain in the open, where she feels safe. She tries to control Will by giving orders. "You take this row," she says, while she passes on to a separate row (121–22).

Throughout this scene, Anna fears closeness and shuns intimacy. Several times the moon seems "to uncover her bosom," causing her to drift emotionally, to lose control of her feelings, but she always recovers. Arriving first at the end of each row, she draws away as Will draws near. And he, responding passively, does what she wants him to. When her sheaves fall down, he picks them up, and he "dutifully" goes where she tells him. "And always, she was gone before he came" (122–23).

After a while, they are working together "in a rhythm," but they do not meet, or come together, as male and female. Instead, there is a space between them, like the space that opens between Ursula and Skrebensky much later in *The Rainbow*. Frustrated, Will exerts his will. He wants to bring Anna close to him, but he cannot. She is far too elusive.

Finally, they do meet, and they kiss. At first, Will responds to her as someone other than himself. For a moment he experiences her as someone new rather than someone he has known all along in his mind. When they kiss repeatedly, he knows that he wants her very badly. Receiving this knowledge in his body "as from a blow," he is overwhelmed. "He had never realized before," Lawrence says, indicating that Will has never made real, in his body, his desire for a woman. Immediately, he is irritated, uncertain, and confused, and he regresses to his earlier, more characteristic self: "Something fixed in him for ever. He was hers." In brief, Will responds passively and gives himself to her once and for all. So when she draws away, he is hurt, feels abandoned, and knows that he has a problem: his dependency. He reacts to this problem by proposing marriage (125).

From Lawrence's point of view, Will is mistaken if he believes that marriage is a solution to the problem of being dependent. Certainly, Lydia and Tom solved some of their problems within marriage. In contrast to Will, they did not leave "it all now, to marriage" (125); they struggled into being after accepting one another as separate and different.

But within the confines of their new house he and Anna cannot ignore their differences or even their separateness for very long. Given that they are individuals with conflicting needs, they begin to battle one another during their honeymoon. The first encounter appears to be minor. "I am dying with hunger," Anna says, and expects to be waited on. Will responds, "So am I," and remains alongside her in bed. When she repeats that she is hungry, he says, "We'll get up," as if they are one person, but neither one moves. She then becomes more emphatic. After resisting briefly and feebly, he gets up, making it appear that it is his decision. "Let me go then," he says (146).

This is a mild encounter and could even be construed as harmless and innocent if it were an isolated or atypical incident, but it is not. To begin with, both Anna and Will act in character; she expects to be fussed over, and he is deferential and passive. Then, too, in this situation, they establish the pattern for their married life together. She makes a demand, he resists and fixes his will for a while, she persists and he gives in. And while it is tempting to credit Will with being loving and kind, it is clear that he does not act from an overflow of positive feeling; he would prefer to remain in bed and be waited on himself. Nevertheless, Will defers to Anna and avoids a conflict. By doing so, he does not have to deal with her as a separate individual or as a woman, so he convinces himself that her request is his desire and that the desire originates within himself. In brief,

Will defers to Anna not because he is kind or wants to preserve a connection with her but because she is strong and he is weak and passive.

His deference preserves the peacefulness of the honeymoon for a while. But when Anna unilaterally decides to give a tea party and causes confusion, she causes a rift. Emphasizing the rift, Lawrence mentions the party in a paragraph in which the words "she," "he," "her," "him," and "his" are used thirty-four times, and the word "they" is used only twice. Clearly, Anna and Will are lining up against one another, and the battle is underway. From now on, it will be "him" against "her" (150–51).

It is pointless, and even impossible, to blame either Anna or Will for what has gone wrong. To begin with, conflict between individuals is inevitable and must be accepted as partially good. Conflict is part of the struggle into being that enables couples such as Tom and Lydia to come through eventually. And, finally, because Will and Anna blame one another in an attempt to shirk their own responsibility, they do not gain from conflict, as Lawrence makes clear in the chapter called "Anna Victrix."

He makes this point several times in chapter 6, but one scene stands out. Anna looks at Will's wood carvings, jeers at his Eve, and says, "Why is she so small? You've made Adam as big as God, and Eve like a doll" (174). Reacting to this accusation, some readers side with Anna and blame Will. But in doing so they ignore something very important: There is no evidence that what Anna says is accurate. It is safe to assume that the male doll is larger than the female and, possibly, is disproportionately large. It is also possible that the female doll is too large, relative to the male. Will does not defend himself and the narrator does not comment on the size of the dolls; therefore nothing is certain except that Anna believes the Adam doll is much too large. But she, like Will, is often subjective. Readers often take sides when they react to this scene, and Lawrence does nothing to discourage them from doing so.

He has a reason for withholding information about the dolls' size; the size really does not matter. What does matter is that Anna and Will repeatedly blame one another for their own failures and limitations to avoid being responsible for their own lives. Often their accusations are accurate. When Will says that Anna is indifferent to him at times and

Anna says that Will is too soulful, both are right. At the same time, both ignore the real cause of their conflicts: within themselves, they do not have surety.

In "Anna Victrix" Lawrence dwells on the inner lives of these two characters, stressing that both have developed one side of their nature and ignored the other: Will is too soulful, and Anna is too sensual. Thus, when he is left out of the preparations for the tea party, Will feels "flayed and uncreated" in his "soul" and, after a while, "the darkness of his soul was thorough" (152). In contrast, Anna responds only physically to what she regards as Will's "negative insensitiveness to her." For example, she often feels physically threatened by Will although he never threatens her physically. Thus his insensitiveness affects her as "something clayey and ugly" (154), like unpleasant flesh. In important ways, then, Anna and Will are opposites.

But the two have something in common. Being only partially developed, each overreacts when the other seems to be a threat. Lawrence uses such words as "hatred" and "tortured" to describe their responses to the most trivial actions. At the same time, he makes it clear that both are subjective. In particular, he uses the word "seemed" repeatedly. According to Will, "She seemed to be destroying him" (172), and, for Anna, he "seemed like a blade of destruction" (177). Anna feels "always attacked" (181), and, when Will relaxes his will at one point, he experiences his condition as "a drowning" (190).

Despite their fear of one another, they do not want to live alone. Will yearns "with passionate desire to offer himself to her, utterly" (155). Of course, he is mistaken to believe that self-sacrifice will result in a vital connection with a woman. Still, when he goes to her, finds her weeping and, feeling pity, makes love, he weeps happily, but he does not understand that "he had yielded, given way" (156). Continuing to respond passively, he convinces himself that her wish originated within him. As a result, he and Anna are "immune in a perfect love" (157) for three days. But the word "immune" is significant—it suggests that they are protected against something. In their house, they are shielded from the outside world and even from one another, for they have not yet begun the struggle into being that would be evidence that they are making progress as male and female.

Will's response to Anna could result in progress. Giving in, he concedes that there "could be only acquiescence and submission, and tremulous wonder of consummation" (156). In Lawrence's fiction, the word "acquiescence" has positive connotations. In keeping with a standard dictionary definition, it means "to rest satisfied" or "to assent to, upon conviction." Lawrence sometimes uses the word "acquiescence" (or some variation of it) to avoid the negative connotations of the word "submission." In *Women in Love,* for example, Ursula acquiesces before she establishes "star-equilibrium" with Rupert,[3] and, in *The Rainbow,* Tom knows satisfaction because he has the strength to acquiesce to Lydia. But Will's response differs from both Ursula's and Tom's, as the use of both "acquiescence" and "submission" suggests. Because these two words have different connotations, the use of them in the same sentence suggests that Will is ambivalent about giving in to Anna. Then, too, he gives in, or yields, without conviction or understanding, and does so slavishly. Because he does not "rest satisfied," as Ursula or Tom would, when he wakes up the next morning, he is slightly depressed and still immune from the world. He has not established an "invisible connexion" with his wife, entered the social world, or resolved the differences that exist between him and Anna.

To emphasize the part Anna plays in their failure to connect Lawrence devotes several pages to focusing on her separateness and lack of connection with everybody, including Will. She is searching for something, Lawrence says, but she is not after what Will wants. She becomes hostile to his beloved church because it emphasizes duty and has nothing to do with the self, which, for Anna, is everything. She wants to know (158), that is, she wants to know mentally rather than realize (make real) through actual experience. Thus she confuses the "thought of her soul" with "the thought of her own self" (159) and, for all practical purposes, makes no distinction between the two; to her, "her soul and her own self were one and the same" (159). Whereas Will cares nothing about his self, Anna believes, and cares nothing for humanity.

For Anna thoughts take precedence over physical reality even though she values material objects and the world of flesh almost exclusively. Thus her thoughts about Will, whether accurate or not, determine her response to him; she despises him because his ideas differ from hers. She resents his interest in "dark, nameless emotion" and his lack of interest in the sermon or in thoughts of any kind. At the same time, because he responds to what she has no knowledge of, she envies him and wants to destroy the "jubilation" of his soul (159). In brief, Anna and Will have ideological differences that open up a great space between them.

These differences become pronounced when they respond to a figure of a lamb in a stained glass window and a photograph of the Pietà in an art book. Anna regards the lamb as silly and self-conscious because she can respond to it only as it appears to the naked eye—a soft, woolly creature that ludicrously holds a flag in one paw. Will ignores entirely what the lamb is literally and seizes on what it symbolizes. Ultimately, the small figure of a lamb is only the body of a lamb for Anna, and for Will the body does not matter at all.

A similar dispute arises when they discuss the Pietà. For Anna, it is only a body that has slits, but "it means the Sacraments, the Bread" (161) to Will. So, again, they clash and, because they are not vitally connected or vitally alive in the flesh, their opposing viewpoints take on excessive importance. What should merely irritate provokes black, violent hatred. Yet, when Anna again weeps and wants to make up, Will reinforces the pattern that has formed; he gives in and makes love, but they are not loving in their lovemaking. He is like a hawk; she is his eager prey. She encourages him to make love viciously and, when he is "satiated," she retaliates against him. But neither experiences satisfaction. To be sure, Lawrence says that Anna is "carried off" by the lovemaking and even says that Will is "satisfied," but he quickly adds "or satiated," which indicates that Will is sensually gratified—temporarily. Almost at once Will is "angry because she had carelessly pushed away his tools so that they got rusty" (163), and she is irritated. Not surprisingly, their battle recurs rather than progresses. After all, they cannot struggle into being by gratifying their senses; instead, they must develop their inner lives.

For Anna, developing an inner life is difficult because she is afraid of any loss of control. When she is looking at the lamb in a stained glass window, she does lose control for an instant. Responding to the influence of the church's tradition, she is "transported to another world. And she hated it, resisted it" (160). Unable to preserve herself and keep her feelings intact, she fights off the conscious knowledge that she is more than the self, or body, that she claims is her entire being; thus she eschews responsibility for having a soul as well as a body. And, to convince herself that she is in the right, she jeers at the lamb and hates her husband for being soulful.

Like Anna, Will refuses to accept responsibility for his inner life, preferring to blame his wife for his limited development. At the same time, he accepts her view that he is foolish for loving the lamb, and, for a while, he hates "the lamb and the mystic picture of the Eucharist" (162). He experiences the hatred as violent and ashy. But almost at once he deflects his anger to Anna. They soon make up and he is "glad to forfeit from his soul all his symbols, to have her making love to him" (162). This time, however, he pays a high price; she breaks something in him. And, because he refuses to "know her" mentally, she deliberately arouses him until he is like a hawk and she, as his victim, is entitled to retaliate. But this hostile approach to lovemaking neither satisfies nor gives them the control they so desperately seek. Instead, they feel threatened and try to preserve themselves by directing darker, more violent hatred at one another.

In the long run, Anna dominates. As the title of chapter 6 indicates, she is a woman who is victorious in a battle. Furthermore, she enjoys her triumph, and Will, "stiff with impotent rage," turns to his wood carvings in order to experience "great satisfaction" in his soul (164). She feels desolate even as she triumphs, and he has "a steady bruise at the bottom of his soul" (165). Nevertheless, they do not make peace for a long time. Consumed by hatred, they decide to "fight it out" (163), and they fight as if they were fighting for existence itself.

Anna, who easily dominates Will in a battle of wills, nevertheless feels his "spell" upon her. Convinced that he is "pulling her down as a leopard clings to a wild cow" (185), she believes that he wants to "devour" her. She even feels "his will fastened upon her" (185) while she is sleeping. Clearly, her response is both subjective and excessive; it reveals more about her than it reveals about Will.

At the same time, Will does exert his will at times. When Anna wants to obliterate him in her own mind, he overreacts. Because he wants her to complete him, his need for her is "like a madness" (179). When she shuns him, he rages "in torment, wanting, wanting" (182). Fiercely dependent, he is extremely sensitive to her every gesture.

F. R. Leavis calls Will's inability to stand alone "a positive trait . . . towards which Anna feels a deep antipathy,"[4] but Lawrence would not agree with him. The title, "We Need One Another," suggests that people do need one another, but there is a difference between mature dependence and immature dependence. Being mature, Tom can admit that he needs Lydia for fulfillment, but he does not follow her like a shadow or feel obliterated when she turns away from him. In contrast, Will is like an infant who has not separated properly from his mother. He does not want to develop into a mature individual who exists in relationship to Anna. Instead, he wants to live through her. So while she wants nothing to do with him for long periods of time, he wants to be rooted in her always.

When Will gives in to Anna, he does not experience "a completeness and an inviolable power" (47) as Tom does when he gives in to Lydia. After all, Tom chooses to acquiesce, acquiesces out of a feeling of fullness and strength, and is met halfway by Lydia who requires no submission. In contrast, Will has no choice, as is illustrated in the scene in which Anna dances naked in her bedroom.

Some critics have interpreted her dancing as positive. To support their claim, they compare her to David who dances naked before the Lord in the second book of Samuel. Anna herself cites David and claims that she is dancing before her Creator. But she is not David. To begin with, she dances because she has no one to rejoice in and is unsatisfied. Then, too, she tries to dance in secret. And, finally, she dances to nullify or "annul" Will. In contrast, David dances in the sight of maidservants, and he dances because he is satisfied and thankful. There is no defiance in his dance, only gratitude. In brief, when Anna's dancing is compared to David's, it becomes obvious that she feels connected to no one or nothing and has no desire to be connected.

When Will accuses Anna of being indecent, their lack of connection is emphasized further. Again, a comparison of Anna and David is instructive. Accused by Michal, David responds affirmatively; he praises the Lord and accepts his connection with the maidservants who have watched him dance. But Anna reacts defensively. "I can do as I like in my bedroom" (185), she shouts, and, feeling that he has fastened his will on her again, she continues the attack. "'What do you do to me?' she cried. 'What beastly thing do you do to me? You put a horrible pressure on my head, you don't let me sleep, you don't let me *live*. Every moment of your life you are doing something horrible to me, something horrible, that destroys me. There is something horrible in you, something dark and beastly in your will. What do you want of me? What do you want to do to me?'" (186). Later, when she repeats the accusation more softly, he replies, "It's something in yourself . . . , something wrong in you" (189). First, he reveals his great dependence on her. She is "everything" to him, even his "derivation." Without her, he will collapse. And he wonders if his deep need for her means that he is "impotent, or a cripple or a defective, or a fragment" (187). So when she makes him sleep on a separate bed in another room, he feels whipped, but he will not leave her. Eventually, he submits quietly rather than face another nocturnal battle. Having no connection with her and lacking inner strength, he cannot tolerate her absence or even her independence. Because he is dependent like "a child on its mother," he "had to give in" (190). Reconciled by doing so, he and Anna become friends, sleep together again, and stop battling, but Will does not feel the vitality in the flesh that, in Lawrences's novels, is evidence of fulfillment as a person and in relationship to other people. He does not feel alive, and there is "a wanness" between him and Anna.

Nevertheless, Lawrence announces that the battle is at least half over at this point. Will has a separate identity, new freedom, and an absolute self; Anna is free of him; they are "very gentle, and delicately happy" (191). But Will's new, independent self is weak, and she has begun to live through her children. Although she is disappointed because the first child is a girl, when she begins to nurse the infant, she looks at her and says, "Anna Victrix." In doing so, she claims victory. Successfully giving birth is part of the victory, but so is the outcome of her battle with Will. He concedes that she is Anna Victrix because he can no longer combat her.

Unable to fight, he is still dissatisfied. He lives for Anna and the children but wonders if he is missing out on something. He is also "troubled in his acquiescence" and vows to stand alone, but he does not believe "in himself, apart from her" (194). So he wonders about a challenge that he may be called to answer, but, for the time being at least, he is unable to do anything or even to move.

Anna, too, remains unfulfilled. Like the Brangwen women of her mother's generation, she strains "her eyes to see something beyond" (195) and sees a rainbow. Although the rainbow suggests hope and reminds her that there is something beyond, she decides not to start on a journey. Convinced that she knows her husband and is "a rich woman enjoying her riches" (196), she allows herself to forget the moon that once beckoned her to follow it. She convinces herself that she "must stay at home now" because she is bearing children (196). So this portion of her life closes as Lydia's did in chapter 3. But Anna is not Lydia. With Tom, Lydia discovers new life. She and Tom do not understand each other mentally, but they have a connection. Thus they pass "through the doorway into the further space" together (95). In contrast, Anna believes she knows her husband mentally and is no "wayfarer to the unknown"; rather, she has already arrived—alone. As Lawrence says, "She was a door and a threshold, she herself" (196).

At the end of chapter 6, the battle between Anna and Will seems to be over; however, Lawrence describes it as only half over. Then, too, because the young Brangwens are still dissatisfied, readers of *The Rainbow* feel some unresolved tension. And, finally, the last words of the chapter direct attention to the future. So Anna's "arrival" and Will's acquiescence are not the end of anything, and the space between chapters 6 and 7 is only an interlude. Soon the battle will resume.

In chapter 7, the battle resumes when Anna and Will visit Lincoln Cathedral. As soon as he refers to it as "she," Anna is ready to fight, and he retaliates when she claims that the faces carved in stone are women's faces. Obviously, neither Will nor Anna has developed very much. A brief visit to Baron Skrebensky's house is filled with reminders that Anna still fears absorption, and Will still wants to absorb himself in other people. Furthermore, Anna has found no "utterance" for her soul, and Will is still too soulful, as the visit to the cathedral emphasizes.

Inside the church Anna is genuinely aroused, but she resists being "transported." Expressing mistrust when her soul is "carried forward to the altar," she is afraid of being swept away and losing control, so she convinces herself that the altar is only "dead matter" (203). In doing so, she preserves herself, but she also foregoes the opportunity to find the utterance that her soul craves.

Will makes a different, but equally serious, mistake; he confuses spirituality and sensuality; he substitutes one for the other. Thus, when his soul goes to "the apex of the arch," he experiences consummation (202). Inside a church, consummation is appropriate because Jesus himself used the word when he was dying on the cross. In this scene, however, consummation is associated with physical responses: ecstasy, touch, clasping, and embracing. Then, too, Will regards Lincoln Cathedral as "the perfect womb" (201), and Lawrence says that the consummation takes place where "the thrust from earth" meets "the thrust from earth" (202). It is clear, then, that Will's consummation is sexual, yet he believes that his soul has been transported.

Witnessing Will's passionate response to the church, Anna becomes resentful. She even jeers at him. She brings to mind an insight she had earlier, namely, "that she did *not* intend her husband to be happy to joy like a fish in a pond" (176). Nevertheless, she is by no means entirely to blame for being hostile toward her husband. He invites her hostility. After all, what she tries to spoil is "his passionate intercourse with the cathedral" (204), not a genuine spiritual response. Then, too, referring back to this portion of his life, Will admits that Anna "had conquered" (207) him. Thus, he acknowledges that he has relinquished responsibility for his own life by the time he visits Lincoln Cathedral. Dominated by his wife, he need only follow her lead. Also, when he claims that she has destroyed his passion for the church, he acknowledges that she has destroyed an illusion. So while it is true that Anna attacks him for loving the church, he is implicated in this attack upon himself. To some extent, he deserves it and, as a passive person, he invites it.

Regardless, the loss of an illusion causes Will to adopt a new attitude toward the church and toward life in general. He now knows that there is life outside the church. He continues to love the church, but only as a symbol. At the same time, his life is becoming more superficial. Having failed to sustain his passionate interest in the church, he remains spiritually "uncreated" and will never develop spiritually because under Anna's influence he begins to live "simply by her physical love for him." Doing so costs him. His soul remains "passionate for something" (208) and, again and again, he consciously submits to Anna. Also, because he knows that "something" is "unformed in his very being" (210), he rages within himself and longs for destruction. Thus, his new attitude affects his inner life negatively but, outwardly, he quietly submits.

Anna responds differently to her battles with her mate. "If her soul had found no utterance, her womb had" (206), so she concentrates on her babies. For her, physical "bliss and fulfillment" are everything. Then, too, because Will serves her, she has some respect for him. For a while the relationship appears to be tranquil, especially after Will centers his life on Ursula, their firstborn. All the while, however, there are danger signals. Will hates his work in the office, begins to suffer from ill health, and is aware that his passion for the church has become barren. It seems only a matter of time, then, before the next explosion.

The next explosion occurs after a period of tranquil indifference. Having acquired the habit of going off by himself, Will picks up a young girl, Jennie, who is, for a short time, "just the sensual object of his attention" (229). Imposing his will on her, he forces her to respond to him sensually. Although they embrace and kiss on a darkened street, the affair does not go very far. Nevertheless, Will is changed by his brief contact with this stranger. When he returns home, Anna notices the change and is fascinated. Almost at once they have sexual encounters that are explosive.

What happens during these encounters and as a result of them is exceedingly complicated. To begin with, the inner lives of Anna and Will are revolutionized. Both feel "liberated" by their new experiences. As Lawrence says, "They abandoned in one motion the moral position, each was seeking gratification pure and simple" (235). They experience sexual intercourse as something that provides intense pleasure. Then, too, they feel free to do "dangerous" and "shameful" things, and Will is free to develop a "real, purposive life" because of what Lawrence calls "his profound sensual activity" (238). But the details of their lovemaking remain a secret, so it is not possible to comment on what transpires as they make love. Nevertheless, it is clear that Anna and Will are influenced by their sexual encounters and equally clear that their relationship has not developed very much even though it has altered radically.

To begin with, Lawrence refers to that relationship as a game, an adventure, and a duel. He suggests that it does not have the "rootedness" that the Tom-Lydia relationship does. Thus, the "gratification pure and simple" that Anna and Will seek is more superficial than the "utter foreignness of contact" (49) that enables Tom to have an "invisible connexion" with Lydia. And although Will is "sensually transported" (236)—and should be—by the sexual encounters, Lawrence is not suggesting that sexual pleasure alone is evidence that a relationship is successful. He emphasizes that sex is the whole relationship between a man and a woman and should not be reduced to sexuality alone.[5] Thus, almost scrupulously, he lists what is missing from the passionate encounters between Anna and Will. There is "no love, no words, no kisses even." There is "no tenderness, no love between them any more" (236). And, without denying that they experience bodily pleasure, he associates that pleasure with violence and death.

Nevertheless, this "maddening intoxication of the senses" (237) could lead to something positive. In particular, it could enable Anna and Will to go beyond themselves to the unknown and to the impersonal love that Lydia and Tom experience. But instead they remain fixated on personal love, on love of the person or body only, and they even regress slightly. They begin to live by one another's standards. Specifically, Will accepts love as something strictly physical, and Anna emulates "the sensual male seeking his pleasure" (235). She decides to do so in her own way, but she is reactive when she decides to be "a free lance" like a man.

Thus she cannot develop her unique, inner life, and he simply ignores his. So they do not grow as individuals, and they do not grow in relationship to one another.

At the same time, they change. Mark Kinkead-Weekes says that they "set each other free,"[6] and Lawrence himself uses the word "revolutionized" to describe what happens to their inner lives. But "revolutionized" means "altered radically" and does not imply progression or change for the better. Then, too, when people are set free, they do not necessarily have direction in their lives and may even become lost. Ursula, for example, is free but finds herself "wandering" through life. So whereas Will is "free to attend to the outside life" (238) and, with Anna, is free from conventional sexual morality, they are only at the beginning of their relationship and their adult lives. What matters is how their inner lives develop over the course of a lifetime.

Lawrence lets his readers know how Anna and Will turn out. Years later, when Ursula is a teenager, Anna is a complacent mother and housewife. She lives through her children and "casts them off" when they become individuals. And, although she is "dominant" in the house, she has not matured. Her "complacent child-bearing had kept her young and undeveloped" (353–54). Having known sexual pleasure and having been altered radically inside, she is, nevertheless, a person who has never struggled into being and gained surety.

Will has been set free to develop a public life and to pursue his love of art, but he is "uncertain, confused." He lives "in connexion with his wife," but there is no evidence that she feels connected to him (354). Rather, her dominance is a reminder that she did not commit herself to him even when he returned from Nottingham and made violent, passionate love to her. "She neither rejected him nor responded to him," Lawrence says. Instead, she threw "everything overboard," including responsibility (235). So, years later, neither she nor Will is "quite personal, quite defined as individuals" (354). They live too much in terms of physical things. Anna has her children, and Will has his work. Eventually, he even has a motor bicycle (425).

Chapter 8

Ursula: Making the Unconscious Conscious

Observed by friends and neighbors, Anna and Will appear normal and even conventional. They do not fight in public or abuse one another physically. Like so many of their contemporaries, they raise a large family (six children), remain married, avoid scandal, make money, and see to it that their children get a good education. Later, when the children are older, Anna is thoroughly domesticated, and Will is a model citizen. Then, too, because they live in a nice house in a good neighborhood, they are successful by the standards of the time.

Despite their success and outward serenity, they are not serene within themselves. They are irritable and insecure and so hostile that they sometimes want to kill each other. Obviously, they are stable enough to control their impulses and hide them from their neighbors. When Will hears Ursula cry for the first time, however, he reveals that something within him is unsettled. Terrified, he does not dare to acknowledge "a deep, strong emotion" that comes "out of the dark of him" (211). When Anna has similar responses to what is dark and unknown, it is clear that she and her husband are not inwardly what they appear to be. By their neighbors' standards, they are not even respectable, for in privacy they engage in what they regard as shameful and unnatural acts.

Nevertheless, this "scandalous" and materially successful couple achieve something that has value. Although they do not struggle into being, as Tom and Lydia do, because they eventually have money, they are free to do something with their lives besides earn a living. Thus, after a twenty-year hiatus, Will returns to his wood carving and begins to develop a purposive life. Then, too, when he and Anna explode out of convention and revolutionize their inner lives, they experience great pleasure in the flesh and are physically satisfied.

At the same time, their success as individuals is only partial. In particular, indulging in sensual pleasure does not lead them to develop their inner lives. Neither unfolds completely, effects a vital connection with another person, or attains to the condition of lasting assurance and satisfaction that Lawrence calls surety. This lack of surety is reflected in their love, which is limited; it has no tenderness and, in fact, is more violent than loving. In keeping with this, when Lawrence describes their connection with one another, he seldom uses the words he uses to suggest that Tom and Lydia have a vital relationship. Rather, when "root," "connexion," "surety," and "flower" appear in the story of Anna and Will, the suggestion is that something is missing from their relationship. For example, Anna feels betrayed into opening like a flower, and she longs for the surety that she does not have. Furthermore, Lawrence begins to use the word "ash" (or some variation of it) more and more often. Thus Anna and Will feel the ashiness of death when they come together in violent lovemaking. So although they do change during their married life together, they do not become complete, sharply defined individuals.

In Lawrence's fiction, individuals who are complete, rather than fragmentary, do not taste the ash of disillusionment in their mouth after they have struggled into being and have established a deep, sustaining connection with a person of the opposite sex. They have new life as a result of assuming responsibility for their own lives. Lawrence says that the germ of *The Rainbow* and *Women in Love* (then called "The Sisters") is "woman becoming individual, self-responsible, taking her own initiative."[1] Yet, as *The Rainbow* illustrates, it is very difficult for either Anna or Ursula to be self-responsible.

There are a number of reasons for this difficulty. To begin with, as time passes and the Brangwens feel cut off from the land, they do not feel part of, or sustained by, anything that is external to themselves. Underscoring this point, Lawrence says that Alfred and the woman from Heanor know from experience "the intercourse between heaven and earth, sunshine drawn into the breast and bowels, the rain sucked up in the daytime" (8). They have a vital connection with the natural world. Two generations later Anna and Will spend a great deal of time indoors. While he is at the office, she is inside a large house and does not stand in the doorway to look out over the fields, as her ancestors did. For both Anna and Will the house is a screen against the outside world of sky and fields (and other people). Neither Anna nor Will derives vitality from nature, as Alfred and even Tom did.

Similarly, successive generations of Brangwens feel increasingly cut off from the community. In contrast to Tom who interacts casually with his contemporaries, both Anna and Will are uneasy when they come in contact with other people. Anna even feels threatened by those who quite naturally have authority over her when she is young, so she deliberately avoids people. When she persuades Will to do the same, both are at ease and, when left alone, feel free to seek sexual pleasure for its own sake. Because they do not feel connected with anyone, including each other, they remain insecure and begin to look for something substantial in their lives. Failing in their search because they fail to look within themselves, they settle for what the eye can see: their bodies, their house, babies, and even gadgets. In doing so, they limit the scope of their lives.

Yet both have an inkling that there is something beyond the senses and beyond themselves. After they explode out of convention, Anna waits for Will's touch as if he is "infinitely unknown and desirable to her," and he discovers "the unknown sensual store of delights" (235–36) that she is. Soon, each ceases to regard the other as the mysterious unknown, and their sensual love becomes strictly personal. Eventually, Will has to see and touch "the perfect place" (237) on Anna's body before it is real to him, and Anna succumbs to her belief that she knows her husband completely because she knows him mentally. When this happens, the doorway into the unknown, which is often half-open to them, closes abruptly.

In the absence of viable community values that could guide them through and beyond the half-open doorway, Anna and Will are, understandably, afraid to venture beyond their life at Cossethay. Unlike Lawrence and Frieda, they are unwilling to become travellers of any sort. Anna asks herself why she should travel and decides that she should stay at home. Sexually unconventional, both she and Will are socially conventional; he has a job in an office and is a model citizen; she raises a large family at home.

Her first child is Ursula, who, like all other people, inherits physical characteristics, personality traits, and even tendencies from her parents. In particular, she has her father's (undeveloped) soul and her mother's sensuality. But she does not grow up in her parents' world. Instead, she moves freely and widely within a community that dissolves as it expands to include all of England and even the continent. Wandering the world, she does not feel bound by social ties and attaches very little value to tradition. By default, the individual becomes inordinately important to her. And, because she does not feel she is a member of the community, she does not accept the role of wife and mother as her inheritance and, even more than Anna, she lives for herself. As an isolated individual, she feels very little responsibility to others, including her family, and feels free to experiment with her life. In doing so, she makes mistakes and even repeats one major mistake when she has a second affair with Skrebensky. She discovers that the man's role in life, which looks so attractive from a distance, is not better than the woman's—nor is it exclusively the man's role any longer. As the community becomes less cohesive, the roles of men and women begin to merge.

As social roles change, so do male-female relationships. Thus Ursula cannot learn what she needs to know simply by applying the past to her modern condition, nor can she rely on the present, for its emphasis on the body and visible objects is misleading. So Ursula must learn a great deal from her experiences. Becoming aware of how she responds inwardly to external events, she must discover that she has a body and a soul and cannot be fulfilled except in relationship with other people.

Ursula: Making the Unconscious Conscious

Fortunately, Ursula is a modern woman who has the freedom to explore alternatives that her parents did not have and her grandparents did not need. But freedom alone guarantees nothing. Ursula's freedom from the restraints of the past makes her aware of her dissatisfaction and is, to some degree, the source of that dissatisfaction. Ultimately, that freedom is even a burden for as she approaches womanhood and realizes that she must make something of her life, she regards self-responsibility as a "cloud." Nor can she ignore the past entirely as she tries to grow: she has to know the past because her life as a girl determines, to an extent, how she experiences life as a teenager and as a young woman. In particular, her father has a great influence on her.

Like Anna, Ursula is her father's favorite. When his second daughter, Gudrun, is born, he bases his life on Ursula. Closely attached to him at an early age, Ursula begins to regard him as almighty and, like many children, feels warm and secure when he is in the house. But he comes too close to her and makes her aware of the need for love and fulfillment too early in life. As Lawrence says, "she was awake before she knew how to see" (221). As a result, her father is a permanent part of her consciousness. Furthermore, he is woven into her dream life, which is largely unconscious, and he influences her as if he exists within her.

Commenting on how powerfully Will affects Ursula, Lawrence emphasizes that magic is important to her and says that "everything her father did was magic" (239). As a child, she nurtures this interest in magic by reading the tales of Andersen and Grimm as well as Tennyson's *Idylls,* which includes stories of romantic love. She also likes the *Odyssey* and the Bible, both of which include magic, or the supernatural. So it is no surprise that as a teenager, her main aspiration is reflected in words from one of these books, the Bible: "The Sons of God saw the daughters of men that they were fair: and they took them wives of all which they chose" (276). During her affair with Skrebensky, Ursula wants to be one of these daughters and wants one of the Sons of God to be her lover.

Ursula eventually modifies her ideal of what the Sons of God are. After she is disillusioned with Skrebensky for the second time, she realizes that she has created a Son of God out of her own desires. Accepting this, she is relieved, for the burden of such a creation is awful. But, first, the stories of magic that she heard as a child influence her. Thus, at first she waits for Skrebensky "like the Sleeping Beauty" (299) and, when she is with him, she is in a "wonderland" and "a magic land" and feels "enchanted" (305). Later in life, she even regards college as "a magic land" (430) for a while. The world of magic and fairy tales has a profound effect on her; and her father is part of that world. Naturally, she responds very strongly to everything he does.

When she is very young and lives a secluded life with Will, her extreme responses barely matter. Soon, however, the outside world intrudes in the form of a charwoman, who scolds Ursula. When Will takes the old woman's side, Ursula feels "the cold sense of the impersonal world" (219) for the first time. Hurt, she begins to withdraw into her own world but continues to love her father, who centers his life on her. Then, one Eastertime, she helps him set potatoes. For Ursula, this is an experience that remains "as a picture, one of her earliest memories" (221). For readers of *The Rainbow* this is important as a reenactment of the scene in which Anna and Will gather sheaves in the moonlight, only this time Will is in control and takes revenge on Anna through Ursula. He tells his daughter what to do, works his separate row, avoids her, tells her to keep her distance, and has "another world from hers" (223). Ursula feels powerless. She is even aware that there is a great gap, or breach, between them. Naturally, she is hurt and disappointed.

This is not the last time Ursula is disappointed in her father, the man who is part of her unconscious dream world. Later, when they are swimming, he terrifies her by dunking her in the water and, on another occasion, he pushes her on a swing until she turns pale and becomes ill. Although she recovers physically, she is permanently affected in her soul. Commenting on this, Lawrence says that "for the first time in her life a disillusion came over her, something cold and isolating. . . . Her soul was dead towards him. It made her sick" (226). At this point, love and disillusionment blend into one another and become a permanent part of her inner life.

Even as a child, Ursula learns to defend herself against this mesh of pain, disappointment, and love. Reacting to her father's cruelty, she establishes a pattern of behavior that influences her relationships with men into adulthood. Bruised in her soul, she wills herself to forget what has happened. She becomes reserved and cuts herself off from the outside world. Disconnected emotionally from other people, she becomes "hard," regards only herself as real, experiences the external world as something vague, and although she is tormented by "the unreality of outside things," she does not mend her ways. After all, she knows from experience that the outside world is cold, impersonal, and evil; she has experienced even her beloved father as "part of this malevolence" (224). Aching in her soul, she is willing to cut off all connections to avoid pain.

Thus, Ursula repeats her mother's mistake; she cuts herself off from the world of knowledge and experience. But she cannot escape from the world of concrete reality and would not be satisfied even if she could. As Lawrence says, "we have a common way, a common interest, not a private way and a private interest only."[2] Thus Ursula needs to interact with other people if she wants to be fulfilled and complete.

After her father wounds her in her soul, she behaves as if she has a body only. Thus, her "adventures" with Skrebensky and Winifred Inger are strictly sensual. And, because she is able to experience extreme sensual pleasure, she indulges herself sexually and avoids any social commitment for as long as she can. But, like Lawrence himself, she has a deeply religious nature and craves the conviction felt in the blood. Because she is by no means sectarian, she wants nothing to do with the visible church after she is an adult. But, eventually, she wants to find out what is "beyond" the flat material world—the world that the eye can see and the mind can know. So she begins to discover her own religion, one that derives from her own experience and continues to evolve in *Women in Love*.

She is often indifferent to—and even hostile toward—the past, especially as it is embodied in her mother. At the same time, the past molds her. The past is not a specific agent that, like gravity, has a predictable effect; it does not compel her to have an affair with Skrebensky or to go to college. Nevertheless, although she criticizes her parents and tries to negate their influence on her, she becomes like them in some ways. Thus, like Anna, she responds to internal threats as if they are external and, again like Anna, she responds to them excessively. Emphasizing this,

Lawrence uses words such as "destroyed" and "always." For example, Ursula feels she will be "destroyed" if she reveals her vulnerability since there is "always the menace against her" (270). So, if Ursula wants to find new life, she will have to rely on her experiences, for conscious intentions cannot transform her inner life and make her different from her parents.

Nevertheless, conscious awareness of alternatives to her parents' life is important. Lydia's stories about the past, "a sort of Bible" (260) for Ursula, suggest alternatives. Listening to her grandmother's accounts of husbands as different as Tom and Paul Lensky, Ursula learns that there are slavish girl-brides who serve their husbands out of love, fear, and duty and discovers, too, that some women have a symbiotic relationship with a man. Learning this, Ursula knows that she can settle for immature dependence or can search for mature dependence, or interdependence, with a man. She has experienced love as a powerless girl dependent on her father, so knowledge of such alternatives is valuable. The world has changed since Lydia was a girl, however, so Ursula cannot simply imitate her grandmother by marrying Skrebensky. Ursula has to struggle to achieve what Lydia did so easily and Anna refused to do: discover what is beyond the world of the senses and the narrow confines of Cossethay.

Even as a girl, Ursula has no standard other than herself and "her own people." Consistent with this standard, she expects everyone to measure up to her parents, her grandmother, and her uncles, who are like her. Soon, however, she is disappointed in "limited people" and wants to go beyond her home town to the vast outside world where she would find people "she would love" (264). When she feuds with her mother and is humiliated by her father, the urge to get away intensifies, but she is trapped. Feeling resentful, she spends a great deal of time by herself and, to justify her resentment, convinces herself that other people are in the wrong. She even develops her mother's habit of criticizing everything other than herself.

Fortunately, she does more than criticize. As Ursula grows older, she learns about herself. To begin with, she discovers that her soul is undeveloped and, later, she realizes that she confuses her soul with material substance. But she is a fighter and has the religious person's great belief in life, so she does not give up easily when external reality conflicts with her ideas. Instead, she struggles to become whole by making the unconscious conscious. To accomplish this she begins to assess her experiences.

Initially, she articulates her position and asks some crucial questions: "How to act, that was the question? Whither to go, how to become oneself? One was not oneself, one was merely a half-stated question. How to become oneself, how to know the question and the answer of oneself, when one was merely an unfixed something-nothing, blowing about like the winds of heaven, undefined, unstated" (284). Like many people, especially the young, she wants answers to questions as basic as "Who am I?" and "What is life?" Listening to her contemporaries, she does not find answers that apply to her. When one of her teachers, Dr. Frankstone, claims that life is merely chemical and physical activity and contains no mystery, Ursula is unconvinced, for she has experienced the nonmental life of the body, which science cannot explain, and, looking through her microscope at school, she sees in the activity of one-celled animals behavior that cannot be explained by forces. So she rejects the belief that only material substance is real, and, like the deeply religious person she is, continues to search for purpose and meaning in her life.

Looking for a purpose, she eventually rejects consciousness as the sole way of knowing. Thus, she takes a step toward valuing the unconscious, which cannot be known mentally. Yet, so many people accept what she rejects: Anna, Dr. Frankstone, Anthony Schofield, Winifred, Uncle Tom, and even her beloved Will. To resist so much authority she has to be a rebel and must go against both family and church. She is confused about God and Jesus for a while and even feels degraded because she confuses "the spirit world with the material world" (287). She reacts to her confusion by testing Christian tenets. When Theresa slaps her, she turns the other cheek. She also considers how she would feel if she gave everything to the poor and became like the despicable Wherrys. In both instances, she listens to her body, which informs her that her mind is wrong. Being a Christian does not make her feel good. Thus, when she is sixteen and realizes that Jesus has been her substitute for physical love, she acknowledges that her approach to Christianity has not worked, for she is still "soulless, uncreated, unformed" (288). So she can no longer rely on the church to give meaning and substance to her life.

Having already rejected her parents' values, especially Anna's belief in "fecundity," she has neither family nor church to rely on and must rely on herself. For her this is difficult because, even as an eleven-year-old child, she hated responsibility. Like Anna, she has learned to handle problems by escaping from them. Thus, it is "torment" for her "to inherit the responsibility" or her own life, but she believes that she must if she is going to make something out of the "nothingness" that she is (283). Commenting on this, she says, "One was responsible to the world for what one did. Nay, one was more than responsible to the world. One was responsible to oneself" (284).

When Ursula comes to this conclusion, she is still a girl and has little understanding of what self-responsibility is. Then, too, she continues to waver and blame others for her failures for a long time. Nevertheless, she has made a start by making an important distinction: She is responsible to the world and, beyond that, to herself; thus she cannot ignore others nor can she simply please them by being conventional, by being successful, or by fostering the right image. Instead, she must discover what has intrinsic value in the world of knowledge and experience.

Naturally, she does not find lasting happiness at once or ever. Instead, like many of Lawrence's strongest characters, she makes many wrong turns before she finds her way. Because she is unwilling and unable to use the past as a guide into the future, she even repeats her parents' mistakes. Paradoxically, she becomes dependent like Will and, like Anna, tries to be independent and dominant. She cuts herself off from vital connection with other people and is free, eventually, "free as a leopard that sends up its raucous cry in the night" (449), that is, she is defiant, brave, hostile, and alone. When she and Anton make love, they revoke the world of people entirely, thus forfeiting the opportunity to grow in the world of knowledge and experience.

When she tries to be perfect, she makes another wrong turn. Nevertheless, for a long time she needs to believe that she is a kind, loving girl who yearns only for "goodness and affection" (323) and, even as a child, she wants only "spirituality and stateliness" (265). She hates the Wherrys, beats a student with a stick, and psychologically annihilates Skrebensky, but she does not admit that she is aggressive by nature and cannot believe that anyone dislikes her. Yet, gradually, she becomes aware of what she and other people are like. Seeing her Uncle Tom curl back his teeth "like an animal," she recognizes that at least some people have a "bestial" side (252). And, because her "starts of revulsion and hatred" are "more inevitable than her impulses to love" (288), she begins to realize that she has something in common with those bestial people; she, too, is aggressive. Yet, for a long time she idealizes herself.

To mature Ursula must relinquish her self-ideal; she finds it difficult to do so because she learned as a child to avoid rather than resolve anything unpleasant. Following up on this practice as a teenager and a young woman, she divides her life into separate sections, for example, family, school, career, and love. Thus, when she is disappointed in love, she can escape by concentrating on her career for a while, and, when teaching disappoints her, she can go to college. Using this strategy, she can avoid self-responsibility for a long time.

Ursula first uses this strategy when as a girl she artificially divides her life into a Sunday world and a weekday world. At the time, she fears that a whole crowd of people wants to pounce on "her undiscovered self" (271). Certainly, her response is subjective, for there is no evidence that anyone is out to get her. Nevertheless, she experiences (feels) the threat within herself, so it seems real to her. Convinced that she needs a haven better than school, which makes her feel only rather safe, she splits off the Sunday world from the rest of the week and, for a while, feels safe on Sundays.

Lawrence records Ursula's response to the Sunday world. At first she associates it with Jesus, excitement, freedom, and escape from the vulgar mob. Soon, however, other people enter her haven, spoiling her bliss, and she becomes critical. Resembling her mother, she objects to the holes in Jesus' feet and rejects any literal reading of the Bible. She reacts against the New Testament emphasis on soul and spirit and wants "marriage in the flesh" only (282). So, finally, religion, Jesus, and the entire Sunday world become unreal, like a story or a myth, Lawrence says. As a result, the weekday world triumphs.

At this critical juncture she meets Anton Skrebensky, who is, for her, what Will was for Anna: an escape. When she is sixteen, she uses him to get away from home and, six years later she uses him to avoid being responsible for her failure in college. In both instances she is also attracted to him because he represents something larger and more important than her narrow, disappointing world and also because he is physically attractive. The first affair leaves her feeling spiritually cold; the second makes her feel dead. So, as a girl and as a young woman, she eventually wants to escape from Skrebensky too.

At the same time, she is reluctant to give him up, for he serves her in several ways. As her lover, he is her tenuous connection with the outside world and a a screen against the world that Ursula believes is a threat to her. When she is twenty-two, she regards him as her last screen against external reality. Having experimented with Jesus, a woman (Winifred), education, and career, she is on her own or, as Lawrence says, she is up against her own fate when her second affair with Anton leaves her feeling dead and disillusioned. Her experiences free but do not fulfill her; rather, they make her feel that she has become a spiritual and emotional "nothing."

Experiencing the emptiness of her existence, Ursula decides that she must modify her soul. To accomplish this, she must become self-responsible, that is, she must develop her entire self if she wants surety and fulfillment. Of course, she could be merely an image, a shell of a human being. If she did so, she would avoid the pain of struggling into being and would certainly succeed in the world, for she is intelligent, educated, strong, and attractive. But, gradually, she would become more and more like Winifred, who is outwardly confident and beautiful but lacks a soul, and so becomes "ugly, clayey" (344). Ursula realizes that she must go beyond Winifred if she wants to avoid her mistress's fate.

To understand Ursula's development, it is necessary to study all phases of her life, including the most destructive ones, and uncover a pattern. Driven by what is unconscious within her, Ursula creates a version of reality out of her own desires. Thus, at irregular intervals, her reality clashes with external reality, and she becomes disillusioned. Each succeeding disillusionment makes her increasingly aware of the void that exists where her soul should be; however, for a long time she ignores what is invisible and concentrates instead on the flat, unrounded world of consciousness and material objects. When this approach no longer works, she must fall back on herself, struggle into being, and allow the kernel (her essential self) to break through the shell of materialism that encloses it. But for Ursula this is not easy. She succeeds eventually, but first she tries to derive satisfaction and fulfillment from two traditional sources: work and love.

Ursula could know in advance that work, or a career, is not necessarily satisfying. After all, her father hates his office job. Then, too, as her father's companion, she must have heard many complaints about jobs. And, finally, when she is a teenager, she maintains that one career, the military, makes a person a "nothing." So Ursula could skip the phase of her life called "career." Yet if she were to do so, she would never feel in her blood what she knows in her mind, namely, that career alone does not satisfy a person's deepest needs. Taking the job at the Brinsley Street School is important to Ursula, for as a teacher she learns that she does not want to be a teacher.

When Ursula begins to teach, she has already been disillusioned with family life, the church, Will, Anton, and Winifred. She regards Will as "null" (331) and feels a "sense of deadness" (344) when she has contact with Winifred. As a result, she wants to avoid closeness with people and tries to escape once more from the world of external reality, which she finds so oppressive.

Having escaped, she soon regards her new residence, the school, as a prison that threatens her. Nevertheless, because she wants to seal herself off from home and the past, she is grimly satisfied when she accepts the school as "the reality" in contrast to Cossethay, which is only a "minor reality" (373), but she also feels oppressed again. Because her role as teacher forces her to live entirely in terms of external things, she soon feels that she is "non-existent" (376) and has "no soul in her body" (377). She even feels as if the school exists within her, where her soul should be. Yet, she responds passively for a while, waiting for the crisis that will set her free.

While she is waiting, the prison becomes worse and worse. She is blamed for the disappearance of pens from her classroom, has to submit to Mr. Harby's authority, and watches Harby beat a student. Reacting to the violence, she becomes ill. Soon, however, she herself beats a student. Challenged by Vernon Williams, a "rat-like boy" (398), she strikes him with a cane until he is broken and blubbering. At this point she becomes part of the physical violence that she loathes and begins to realize that she, like other people, is capable of aggression. Becoming conscious of this, she suffers. Because her hands touched Vernon, she feels violated and pays "a great price out of her own soul" (405) when she is forced, later, to beat other boys.

Teaching does not give her pleasure and being free does not satisfy her. Instead, as she gains freedom, she becomes aware of how discontented she is and realizes that she is looking for something she cannot define. At times she seems to know that that something is not only beyond her but deep inside. More often, however, she behaves as if she can satisfy herself by living for external things only.

Disillusioned again, she considers returning to Skrebensky but is unwilling to give up "the working world" (410). Besides, she believes that there is more than one man for every woman, so she is opposed to marriage. It becomes clear that Ursula is not committed to any one person or any one thing. She favors something called joy, but joy is merely an abstraction, an ideal condition, so she has no aim or direction and is dissatisfied. Nevertheless, she continues to struggle against what seems to confine her. Unlike Maggie Schofield, whose life encloses her eventually, Ursula will not give up.

At this point in her life, it is important that Ursula be a rebel who refuses to adopt conventional views of love and marriage for during one of her holidays Anthony Schofield proposes to her. Anthony would be a pleasant husband; he is decent, dependable, deferential, and attractive. Then, too, because teaching is such a strain for Ursula, marriage would be a convenient escape. But Anthony has no soul, Ursula decides (416), so she rejects him. As a result, the doorway into the beyond remains open. In contrast to Anna and Will, Ursula has a chance to become a differentiated individual who eventually unfolds and becomes a complete person.

Nevertheless, she clings to the past and creates dreams about the future even after she rejects Anthony. She prepares herself for another disillusionment when she goes to college, for nothing in the present world of concrete reality can match memories or dreams created out of her own desires. Because she has dreamed about a college, she experiences the actual campus and buildings as both "remote" and "magic" (430) and, for a while, idealizes knowledge, the professors, and the school's beauty. With two years of college remaining, school no longer seems glamorous to her, and Ursula reverts to criticizing everything. She echoes Lawrences's sentiments when she describes the college as commercial and the professors as peddlers of other people's ideas. Nevertheless, she reveals something unstable and incomplete in herself when she looks ahead and sees through doorway after doorway only "another ugly yard, dirty and active and dead" (436). Unable to feel vital and alive within herself, she projects her own deadness onto the outside world and into the future.

Significantly, Winifred, college, and the future begin to merge in Ursula's mind and all three are associated with disillusionment. Because she is disappointed in school and her mistress, she anticipates disappointment in the future. Underscoring this point, Lawrence again uses the word "ash." Ursula can taste ash in her mouth and feel its grit between her teeth. She even experiences the "grey ashiness" (438) of everyday existence within herself. Thus, when she begins to think about herself, she is "always negative" (437), for she has become a negative person inside.

She has a positive side, but it is "like a seed buried in dry ash" and is "dark and unrevealed" (437), that is, Ursula is unaware of it for she lives exclusively in the lighted world of consciousness. Even as she looks at what gleams and glimmers in the darkness, she avoids the darkness itself, where the core, or seed, of her self exists.

To avoid or block out the dark, unconscious part of herself, in her second affair she tries to live through Skrebensky, whom she associates with brightness and radiant light. He is another of her dreams, the doorway into a happier future and the embodiment of complete (or perfect) love. Thus, when she receives his letter, she is excited because she believes that he can be her life and even "the nucleus to the new world" (442). Yet, as she contemplates a second affair with him, she experiences more pain than pleasure and can no longer be spontaneously happy. She feels only "old" excitement (439), so when she decides to become Anton's lover again she is regressing.

To understand what happens during her second affair, it is necessary to understand the first, which begins when she is still a girl. Aware of the fact that she has used Jesus as a screen against the world, she looks for his opposite when she seeks a lover and settles on Anton. He is, after all, very sensual, and he has no soul. But Ursula uses him the way she used Jesus. Making him her new screen against the world, she seizes him "for her dreams" (292). She is thrilled and assumes she is in love, but Lawrence says she is merely in love with "a vision of herself" (293). He indicates that she is excited because she is defying her parents and is locked in a battle of wills with her lover. Yet, because she believes she is in love, she can justify her domination of Skrebensky until she becomes, finally, Ursula Victrix.

Before her ultimate victory, Ursula has a romantic relationship with Anton. Glowing inside, she responds to him as something shiny, is intoxicated with his kisses, and feels that she is in an enchanted land. But her responses are superficial—she is thrilled equally by his kisses and his car. And, because thrills do not provide lasting satisfaction, she soon yearns for something deeper in "her soul" (306).

Yearning and dissatisfied, she becomes hostile and picks a fight with Anton on the subject of soldiers and war. During their fight, both reveal how tenuous their relationship is. Like Anna and Will, they cannot tolerate the tension that results from ideological differences. Anton is defensive; Ursula tells him that he is nothing to her. When he disagrees with her, a feeling of "hard separateness" comes over her; he puts distance between them by intellectualizing (310). Unable to connect mentally, neither Anton nor Ursula feels any connection at all.

Lawrence underscores the lack of connection by contrasting Ursula and Anton to the couple on the boat called the *Annabel*. Disagreeing on a name for their baby, the wife calls the husband pigheaded, and he smiles maliciously and refuses to give in to her. But instead of being driven apart by their disagreement, they respond like Alfred and the woman from Heanor. Unflustered by name-calling and abusive smiles, they do not become hard and separate. Skrebensky envies the man because he can worship a woman "body and soul together" (316) even while they are quarreling. The couple on the boat have an "invisible connexion." In contrast, Anton and Ursula have a mental connection only.

In another scene Lawrence uses the moon to emphasize the lack of connection between Ursula and her lover, thus bringing to mind Anna's response to the moon when she and Will are gathering sheaves. Anton, like Anna, is frightened by the moon. In contrast, Ursula yearns for the moon's "coolness and entire liberty and brightness" (319). Anton covers her with a large cloak to protect her from the moon, but thwarted by his gesture, Ursula is filled with destructive rage. Afterwards, she lets Anton exert power over her. As Lawrence says, "She even wished he might overcome her" (320).

Skrebensky, of course, is willing to oblige her, for he is like Ursula in that he wants to win a battle of wills. He wants to trap her and then enjoy her. But kissing her is "like putting his face into some awful death," and closeness with him makes her want to "tear him and make him into nothing" (321). So they battle one another until he yields and feels "consumed" and "annihilated." Having relinquished his will to the great power of her will, he becomes "nothing" (322).

When Ursula reduces Anton to nothing, she is appalled by her capacity for psychological violence. Nevertheless, she wants to continue to believe that she is good, so she simply denies what has happened. Going one step further, she vows not to remember or even to imagine that what she has done is possible. "She was good, she was loving" (322), she tells herself. Yet, for a moment she is conscious of having destroyed Anton, so she tries to recover her former "warm self" by being kind to him and becoming his "adoring slave" (323). But he has changed; he no longer has a core. And, because she knows she has broken him, her soul becomes "empty and finished" (323), and she can no longer successfully repress, block out, or deny all conscious knowledge of her ability to be cruel and hostile.

Reacting to what she now knows about herself, she begins to rebel against everything physical. In her soul she mocks the idea that animals should multiply and replenish the earth, and she rejects a God who is no better than maggots that destroy flesh; nor can she love Anton's body in a tender, friendly way any longer. Because she is frightened by all strong feelings, she becomes a romantic lover whose feelings and professions of love are superficial. She even exchanges photographs with Anton and accepts his ring. Both he and she are elated and can deny what is unconscious, but both have been bruised in their souls and, beneath the thin veneer of elation, Ursula feels a "deep, ashy disappointment" (327).

Using "duty" as a screen, Skrebensky can escape from his desolation and hide behind what he believes in: his country, material prosperity, and personal gratification. But none of these beliefs has intrinsic value, and each distracts him from his inner life, which becomes emptier and emptier. Reacting to his emptiness, Ursula, too, feels "almost extinguished" (329) and is miserable. As Lawrence says, commenting on the final effect of her first affair, "her sexual life flamed into a kind of disease within her" (333).

When Lawrence describes Ursula's sexual life as "a kind of disease," he suggests that something has gone seriously wrong within her: she is paying the price for repressing too much. From day to day, she feels safe and can preserve a good opinion of herself, but in the long run she remains discontented and feels fragmented. Nevertheless, she does not assume responsibility for what has gone wrong in her life. Instead, she blames Anton for everything and wants nothing to do with him. She tries harder than ever to be free from all connections, for anyone who is not a reflex of herself arouses hostility within her. At the same time, she wants a lover because she craves physical satisfaction. Faced with the dilemma of needing what she does not want, she falls in love with someone who is superficially very much like herself, Winifred. She and her teacher are so much alike that their lives fuse and become one (341). Soon, however, Ursula is revolted by her sexual contact with a woman, a feeling that Lawrence emphasizes by using the word "nausea" (343). So, although the two women love one another physically, Ursula rejects Winifred.

In some ways, Ursula's lesbian relationship is destructive. It leaves her feeling more disillusioned than ever and fills her with repugnance for human flesh. Yet contact with Winifred contributes to Ursula's development. For example, when the two women discuss religion, men, marriage, morality, and the Women's Movement, Ursula learns a great deal.

Using this knowledge, she is able to sort our her feelings and make sense of her experiences.

She discovers that loving one's self in another person results in a feeling of deadness and learns, too, that Winifred's apparently unconventional attitudes hide her real values. For example, Winifred severely criticizes men who no longer care about anything, including themselves and marriage, but then marries such a man. As Ursula listens to the heartless dialogue of her Uncle Tom and her mistress, everything becomes "grey, dry ash, cold and dead and ugly" (351), for she realizes that like Winifred she has been attracted to a man who has no soul and cares nothing about himself. Lawrence says that Ursula grows up during her two weeks at Wiggiston, where Winifred and Tom meet, that Ursula realizes she requires something beyond an Anton or a Winifred and beyond the flat, material world.

At the same time, she does not know what it is she requires, so she experiments with her life before she has her second affair with Anton. As a student and as a teacher, for example, she rejects some options but does not find new ones, nor does she do what she must do if she wants to develop as a person: accept responsibility for her own inner life, including her aggression. In continuing to blame others when she finds it difficult to interact with people in the outside world, Ursula does not struggle into being and feel satisfaction. Thus, when college loses its glamour for her, she again tastes the "ash of disillusion" (436) in her mouth and tries to escape from her condition. But she cannot because it exists within her, in her soul. Besides, she still lives in the lighted area of consciousness, ignores what is dark and unconscious, and has no direction in her life.

Feeling isolated and directionless, she hears from Anton and, at once, wants to return to him. For her, he is still associated with light and dreams and is an escape from the grayness of everyday existence. Yet, as soon as they meet, it is obvious that neither Ursula nor Anton has developed since their first affair, for their relationship begins exactly where it left off. After a six-year separation, they are still enemies. Anton has not regained his confidence or developed his inner life; rather, he has "sidetracked" his soul and, abjectly, wants to give himself to her. He even kneels in front of her, "exposing himself" (443). He is physically appealing, so Ursula takes him for "her satisfaction" (444), as she did six years earlier. But this time she knows, beforehand, that she has power over him. By rejecting him, she could cause something to "die in him" (443).

Aware of her potential to be destructive to Anton, Ursula has to work harder than ever to keep the unconscious hidden from consciousness. She must distance herself not only from Anton but also from other people since interaction with people makes her aware of her own aggression. Believing that "all must be kept so dark, the consciousness must admit nothing" (443), she develops a mocking, jeering attitude and keeps her distance from people who pass in the street. After a while, she is indifferent even to the most superficial connection with others and in a burst of triumph decides that her "social self" can "look after itself" (452).

When Ursula rejects her social self, she believes that she and Anton have become a world unto themselves (456). However, Ursula is unable to sever her connection with the outside world completely—for example, she worries about her appearance when she attends lectures at the college. Then, too, when she runs naked in the woods, in defiance of civilization, she wears sandals, a tenuous but tangible reminder that she is not disconnected from everyday life and ordinary people.

She also begins to grow beyond her immature dependence on convention, career, education, and even other people. As she does so, she feels strong and begins to accept responsibility for "the darkness" that is within her; when she goes beyond "her temporal, social self," she feels that she has "never been more herself" (452). At this point, she is evolving as an individual who accepts responsibility for her entire life.

Accepting responsibility means refusing to imitate her parents, grandparents, and contemporaries. She does not need to reject marriage and children, but she must marry for individual, not conventional, reasons. Lawrence illustrates that accepting responsibility also means making choices and living up to them when he presents Ursula with two contrasting options as she sits at the top of the downs near Dorothy York's cottage. From her vantage point she can see the Channel and a river winding its way to the sea, but she can also see the villages and a train moving aimlessly across the countryside. Following the river, Ursula could travel and move physically away from the life that restricts and confines her, or, going down into the village, she could return to a past that does not fit the present or apply to her life. As readers of *The Rainbow* know, she chooses to travel.

Ursula should not be commended simply because she travels. Her motive for traveling reveals that something within her is still unsettled and incomplete. Lawrence says that she craves novelty and wants to move on even in the middle of a sunset. Although traveling is, in part, a nervous reaction on Ursula's part, nevertheless, as an immature girl she uses travel to escape from what she depends on excessively. In particular, she can get away from Skrebensky, who, at Rouen, feels the coldness of death while she sinks "into apathy, hopelessness" (456). Regardless of her motive, it is important that she move on.

Yet, for a long time, she wanders toward death and, perversely, clings to Skrebensky even though she observes him becoming "fixed and stiff and colourless" (457). His attachment to her is even more perverse: her absence destroys "his being" (457). And, because he lacks a soul or any inner life, and because he is immature, he is totally dependent on her. He is so dependent that he cannot tolerate any uncertainty about his connection with Ursula; either he must have her or be rid of her entirely.

Lawrence makes clear why Skrebensky is so dependent. Because he can respond only to the "cold surface of consciousness" (458), he is not vitally connected to anything and, consequently, cannot develop an inner life. As Lawrence says, he has "no being, no contents" (458) and is only an empty shell that incorporates physical objects within itself in order to overcome the feeling of emptiness. He even appropriates Ursula. All the while, of course, he continues to lack surety and, as a result, experiences any rebuttal of his desires or thwarting of his wishes as a threat. So when Ursula says bluntly that she is against him, he feels sickness and even death. Contact with her is so overwhelming that he has to struggle to feel that he exists. And when she accuses him of not satisfying her sexually, he is filled with rage and wants to kill her (462–63).

Ursula knows that he is a void inside, that he cannot connect with anyone, but she does not sever her connection with him, for he suits her needs; he serves her and is "a screen for her fears" (465). Besides, she likes his body and even feels that she owns it. So she allows him to make love to her, but their lovemaking, like Anna and Will's, is cruel and hostile and contains a "germ of death" (463).

Ursula and Skrebensky do not respond in the same way to their vicious lovemaking. Madly dependent on her and unable to arouse her, Skrebensky is "savagely satisfied" and "revenged" (477) but grows deader and deader inside. Eventually, even her kisses make him feel helpless and afraid. She seems to have a "beaked mouth," so when she pins him down to her chest as they make love, he feels not merely dead but as if he will be motionless forever (480). He has "a new access of superficial life" in the morning, but he has no soul or background and knows his will is broken. Expressing his psychological reaction as if it were physical, Lawrence says that Anton would be "obliterated" and his bones broken if he were to see Ursula again (481).

Ursula's response to their lovemaking is also destructive in some ways, but her response ultimately differs from Anton's. As Lawrence says, "She was in some other land, some other world, where the old restraints had dissolved and vanished, where one moved freely, not afraid of one's fellow man, nor wary, nor on the defensive, but calm, indifferent, at one's ease" (472).

Having become disillusioned with virtually everything that traditionally gave meaning to a person's life, she must rely on herself ultimately, or die. Therefore she rejects what her contemporaries regard as love because it is too personal and does not lead anywhere. But she cannot simply become promiscuous, for promiscuity is a continuation of the behavior that makes her taste ash in her mouth; far from being a cure, her lack of sexual commitment is evidence that something has gone wrong within her. So she cannot settle for Anton, who seems "outside her" (473), and cannot search for lovers randomly and indiscrimanently. Then, too, because she has broken the "bonds of the world," she is up against her own fate and must seek new life: a "connexion with the unknown" (474).

Like Anna, Ursula yearns for the unknown. Anna does not make the unconscious conscious; instead, she settles for what is known and, as a result, is not sharply defined as an individual in middle age. In contrast, Ursula is concerned as a young woman because she is "not pronounced enough" (476). And, because she has experienced what Anna only yearns for and knows mentally, Ursula discovers that there is more to life than the physical world. Acknowledging that this "more" is within her, in the darkness of her unconscious, she begins to make the unconscious conscious, and she makes a crucial decision to "modify her soul" (472).

Chapter 9

Ursula: The Search for New Life

When Tom kisses Lydia in the vicar's kitchen, he is "newly created." Both he and Lydia experience a "new life" (46) and, two years later they discover the "new world." Passing through "the doorway" into their new life, they feel the "bonds and constraints" of the material world, but they also experience "complete liberty" (95–96). After all, they are separate, rooted together, and at ease in the world of physical objects.

A generation later, Anna and Will experience great bodily pleasure but are not vitally connected to one another. As a result, their relationship is limited. Lawrence says that Will exists apart from Anna, and she is "not quite fulfilled." When she looks at a rainbow and sees the "hope" and "promise" that it suggests, she decides not to venture beyond her present, rich life (195–196), and Will succumbs to her wishes. Consequently, neither he nor she has the "new life" that Tom discovers with Lydia and that Ursula yearns for at the end of *The Rainbow*.

Although she yearns for new life, Ursula has no guidance. She cannot imitate her parents and find fulfillment and, because the world has changed so much, she cannot learn from her grandparents. She must discard the past, including Skrebensky and traditional love, even though doing so is painful. Ursula is "inert, without strength or interest" and feels that her energy is "frozen" when she rejects Anton. She also has a conflict. Believing that she is pregnant, she is thrilled in the flesh but "sick" in her soul, Lawrence says (484). Yet, in the long run, her conflicts and suffering pay off because she "comes through" to new life eventually.

To come through (like Lawrence and Frieda, Tom and Lydia), Ursula must be conscious of how much the past influences her even after she rejects it. Like a husk, the past may not nourish, but it continues to enclose her. Then, too, because the past is as safe and comfortable as an old habit, Ursula is reluctant to give it up entirely. Thus, she sometimes regresses by imitating her parents and accepting their values. To justify such inconsistent behavior, she rationalizes it. For example, she tries to convince herself that she has been wrong to want freedom and fulfillment and that she should settle for being Anton's "good" and "dutiful" wife. She even tells herself that Anna is "radically true" and "profoundly right." So, temporarily, she submits to the "bondage" of conventional marriage, which she conveniently calls peace (484–85). When she discovers that pregnancy does not cure her ailing soul, however, she knows that marrying for sex and procreation will not give her the satisfaction she craves. As Ursula submits to the idea that she should become conventional, she feels "the seething rising to madness within her" (486) and makes a conscious decision to reject Anton with whom she has only a physical relationship.

Reacting to the need for satisfaction that includes but also goes beyond the body, Ursula is confused and begins to wander until she comes to Willey Water, where the atmosphere is "free and chaotic" (486), like Ursula herself. Feeling like a bird among a host of warriors, she suddenly senses the presence of some horses. Significantly, she is aware of the horses before she sees them, for they act on her like a force that the eye cannot see. Yet, she resists their influence. Still bound by her old habits, she does not want to know that they exist and, to avoid self-responsibility, wants to "escape" or "circumvent" them. When the wild animals are "up against her," Lawrence reminds his readers that Ursula is "up against her fate," referring to this experience as "the crisis" for Ursula (489).

During the crisis, Ursula is "dissolved like water" (489). Like Tom who lets himself go with Lydia and feels "the tension, the withholding" (95) relax in him, she relinquishes her hard, fixed will. But she differs from her grandfather. When he relaxes his will, he flows toward another person and establishes an "invisible connexion." In contrast, Ursula becomes "like a stone" (490) and cannot develop an inner life because she has no vital relationship with anyone or anything. In fact, whereas Tom experiences "new life" when he acquiesces, Ursula realizes how empty she is inside, in her soul.

In an essay called "Morality and the Novel," Lawrence discusses the need to have relationships in order to develop the soul. "This is how I 'save my soul,'" he says, "by accomplishing a pure relationship between me and another person, me and other people, me and a nation, me and a race of men, me and the animals, me and the trees or flowers, me and the earth."[1] Because Tom has some of the relationships that Lawrence cites, he has developed his soul to the extent that he does not feel annihilated inside by close contact with a woman. Thus, when Lydia's kiss takes him beyond himself (Lawrence uses the word "obliterated" to describe his feeling), Tom quickly recovers and returns, with ease, to reality. In contrast, when Ursula is unconscious and then becomes vaguely aware of her very tenuous connection with the external world, she feels a "deep, cold sense of nausea." She even dreads being spoken to or speaking. When she realizes that she will have to plod wearily through the world for the rest of her life, she becomes ill for two weeks (490–91).

Possibly Ursula wants to be ill so that she can avoid entanglement in the difficult world of knowledge and experience, but as she lies "shaken and racked" in her bed, she discovers "firmness of being" and "dependency" within herself (491). She realizes that her connection with Skrebensky is false and shallow. She still feels bound to him because of the baby she believes she is carrying, but she tries to separate herself from him. She disentangles herself from all feeling, from her own body, and from everyone she knows. She even tries to convince herself that she does not belong in the "world of things" (492–93), where Anton exists.

When Ursula tries to separate herself from "her father, and her mother, and her lover, and all her acquaintance" (492), she makes another in her series of mistakes. But by doing the wrong thing first, she learns what she wants to reject. In fact, she begins to affirm life when she realizes she is a kernel "striving to take new root" (493). Lawrence invites a comparison of Ursula with Anna, for whom Will becomes the "kernel of life" (130), whereas Ursula is the kernel itself. Thus, if Ursula wants to grow, she cannot live in a world that is "a bygone winter," (493) nor can she live through a man or even a baby.

Of course, when she regards the kernel as "the only reality" and everything else as "husk and shell," she is responding subjectively. After all, Anton's body, the countryside, the factories, and even gadgets do exist and have a real influence. But because Ursula experiences them as unreal, she has no choice; she must break "like a nut from its shell" (493), for the shell of the material world prevents her from going beyond what is visible. Anton's body and sexual pleasure itself are only dead ends that do not lead to her growth and satisfaction. As Ursula said to Dorothy York earlier, "So much personal gratification. It doesn't lead anywhere" (475).

Drawing attention to the need for growth in Ursula and her contemporaries, Lawrence uses the word "new" repeatedly in the last pages of the novel. For example, he cites "new ground," "new root," "new knowledge," "a new Day," "new dawn" (493), "a new liberation" (494), and a "new germination" (494, 495). When Skrebensky informs Ursula that he is married and she responds emotionally, she realizes that she has not cut herself off from her old life completely. Nevertheless, she looks ahead instead of back and sees "a new creation." As Lawrence says, "In everything she saw she grasped and groped to find the creation of the living God, instead of the old, hard barren form of bygone living" (495).

Rejecting the old form and embracing newness, Ursula is not whole and satisfied all at once. Instead, she is "sick with a nausea so deep that she perished as she sat" (495). But unlike Will, who remains a bud, and Anna, who cannot unfold, Ursula begins to grow; she is a flower. That flower is fragile and is associated with winter, but it is unfolding and lets in the "new dawn" (493). Gaining strength as a day gains strength, Ursula can go beyond Anton, who is "that which is known" (494), to the unknown, undiscovered world that lies ahead, thus developing the permanency, or surety, that she felt within herself as she lay ill.

When Lawrence stresses the importance of inner strength, he is not suggesting that the life of the body is unimportant. Quite simply, body and soul are not mutually exclusive. According to Lawrence, the two are interdependent. Ursula, however, is like so many modern people in that she takes for granted the reality of the body and ignores the soul. Intent on convincing people that this one-sidedness has negative effects, Lawrence emphasizes that new life is not possible for individuals or the human race unless the body is in league with the soul.

A month before he submitted the final version of *The Rainbow* to Methuen, Lawrence wrote a letter in which he commented on the soul's relationship to the body. Stressing that people's souls would be "so maimed and so injured" after the war, he continues to be "big with hope for the future." He also cites the need for each individual to "fulfill his own nature and deep desires to the utmost" and to accept "the intrinsic part" of people as "the best part." Eschewing abstract principles and outmoded habits, he says that the "ideal, the religion, must now be *lived, practised*. We will have no more *churches*." Continuing to stress "the new hope" for the future, he accepts that the "present community . . . simply can't go any more." As a result,

> It is no good plastering and tinkering with this community. Every strong soul must put off its connection with this society, its vanity and chiefly its fear, and go naked with its fellows, weaponless, armourless, without shield or spear, but only with naked hands and open eyes. Not self-sacrifice, but fulfillment, the flesh and the spirit in league together, not in arms against one another. And each man shall know that he is part of the greater body, each man shall submit that his soul is not supreme even to himself.[2]

As a comment on a work in progress, this letter is excellent. It is a summary of Lawrence's conscious intentions as he put the finishing touches on his novel, and makes explicit the author's belief that people must reject what has become husk, especially the church and what society has come to be in the modern world. But Lawrence affirms much that is positive: the intrinsic self, a religion that is lived (practiced), the body and the soul (when they are working together), and the quest for "a new community which shall start a new life."[3] In brief, the letter is evidence that Ursula's conduct in the last chapter of *The Rainbow* is meant to lead to new life if she perseveres.

Obviously, she has not found "a new community" to take the place of the one she discarded. Instead, she is alone and, early in *Women in Love,* has difficulty existing in relationship with anyone, including Rupert Birkin. As she is "striving to take new root" (493) she is not like the woman of Heanor who, with Alfred, lives separately but from "one root" (13), for she has not yet established star-equilibrium with a man. When Lawrence says that Ursula has "her root in new ground" (493), he makes it clear that she lives in a world different from that of the woman of Heanor. The fields are covered with factories and coal mines, the sky is filled with smoke, and the people do not have Alfred's or Tom's "stable ego." So she has to discover new life within herself if she wants to be vital in the future.

Using the image of the rainbow, Lawrence reinforces the point that Ursula may discover new life. Significantly, the rainbow does not appear in the beautiful, enchanted land that Ursula dreamed about as a girl. In a sketch that Lawrence sent to a friend on 2 March 1915 (the day he sent the final version of his novel to Methuen) and in *The Rainbow* itself, the colored bow rests "in the corruption of new houses" (495); but its arch touches heaven. Clearly, the rainbow symbolizes the marriage of heaven and earth and, within the individual, the marriage of soul and body.

When Ursula responds to the rainbow without rejecting it, she reveals that she has begun to accept the need to grow in body and in soul and to do so in a world of unideal people. Thus she brings to mind her earlier response to the God who sent Noah a rainbow as "a token of a covenant" in the first book of the Bible. Responding to God's promise that he will never again send a flood that destroys "all flesh," Ursula jeers and rejects what she regards as the "lord of flesh." Nor can she find in the rainbow or in the story itself anything that applies to her. As Lawrence says, "She was surfeited of this God" (325–36). But at the end of the novel the rainbow, which comes "from nowhere," makes her hopeful not only for herself but for "the sordid people" who are part of the "world's corruption." Because she is no longer cynical, she sees in the rainbow the promise that "the old, brittle corruption of houses and factories" will be swept away and replaced by a new world (495–96). In that new world she will find new life.

Notes

Chapter 1

1. *The Letters of D. H. Lawrence,* ed. James T. Boulton, 8 vols. (Cambridge: Cambridge University Press, 1979–19–), 2:174.

2. Ibid., 2:205.

3. Ibid., 2:146.

4. Ibid., 2:428.

5. Ibid., 2:268.

6. Ibid., 3:142.

7. Charles L. Ross, *The Composition of "The Rainbow" and "Women in Love": A History* (Charlottesville: The University of Virginia Press, 1979), 29.

8. *The Letters of D. H. Lawrence,* 1:459.

9. Ibid., 1:465.

10. Ibid., 2:212.

11. *Study of Thomas Hardy,* in *Phoenix: The Posthumous Papers of D. H. Lawrence,* ed. Edward D. McDonald (New York: Viking Press, 1936). A large portion of this volume is a survey of Western painting and literature and seems to have little to do with Hardy. If Lawrence intends to demonstrate that Hardy is the end product of a tradition of art that increasingly stresses the abstract, however, everything in the *Study* is germane.

12. *Study of Thomas Hardy,* 487.

13. Ibid., 439.

14. *The Rainbow* (New York: Viking Penguin, 1987), 484; further references appear in parentheses in the text.

15. Mark Kinkead-Weekes, "The Marble and the Statue," in *Twentieth Century Interpretations of "The Rainbow,"* ed. Mark Kinkead-Weekes (Englewood Cliffs, N. J.: Prentice-Hall, 1971), 106. This essay appears in expanded form in *Imagined Worlds, Essays in Honor of John Butt,* ed. Ian Gregor and Maynard Mack (London: Methuen, 1968).

16. *The Letters of D. H. Lawrence,* 2:161.

17. *The Complete Poems of D. H. Lawrence,* ed. Vivian de Sola Pinto and Warren Roberts (New York: Viking Press, 1964), 191.

18. "John Galsworthy," in *Phoenix,* 540.

19. *Study of Thomas Hardy,* 419.

20. Ibid., 410.

21. *The Letters of D. H. Lawrence,* 1:40.

22. Marvin Mudrick, "The Originality of *The Rainbow,*" in *A D. H. Lawrence Miscellany,* ed. Harry T. Moore (Carbondale: Southern Illinois University Press, 1959), 69.

23. Ibid., 75.

24. *Study of Thomas Hardy,* 496.

25. *The Letters of D. H. Lawrence,* 3:143.

Chapter 2

1. *The Letters of D. H. Lawrence,* 2:67.

2. Ibid., 1:544.

3. Ibid., 2:183.

4. Ibid., 2:405.

5. Ibid., 2:479.

6. Ibid., 2:184.

7. Alan Friedman, *The Turn of the Novel: The Transition to Modern Fiction* (London, Oxford, New York: Oxford University Press, 1966), 132.

8. Ibid., 145.

9. Thomas Hardy, *Jude the Obscure* (New York: New American Library, 1961), viii.

Chapter 3

1. *The Letters of D. H. Lawrence,* 2:183.

2. Ibid., 1:526.

3. H. M. Swanwick, review in the *Manchester Guardian,* 28 October 1915; reprint in *D. H. Lawrence: The Critical Heritage,* ed. R. P. Draper (New York: Barnes & Noble, 1970), 98–99.

4. Clement Shorter, review in *Sphere,* 23 October 1915; reprint in *The Critical Heritage,* 96.

Notes

5. James Douglas, review in *Star*, 22 October 1915; reprint in *The Critical Heritage*, 93.

6. Catherine Carswell, review in the *Glasgow Herald*, 4 November 1915, reprint in *Critical Heritage*, 100.

7. "Prosecution of *The Rainbow*," in the *Times*, 15 November 1915; reprint in *Critical Heritage*, 102.

8. Eugene Goodheart, *The Utopian Vision of D. H. Lawrence* (Chicago: The University of Chicago Press, 1961), 5.

9. F. R. Leavis, "D. H. Lawrence" (Cambridge: The Minority Press, 1930), 12, 14, 20, 23.

10. F. R. Leavis, *D. H. Lawrence: Novelist* (New York: Simon and Schuster, 1955), 305, 307, 310, 311.

11. Ibid., 144.

12. Ibid., 97, 99–100, 102, 103.

13. Ibid., 103, 140.

14. Mark Spilka, *The Love Ethic of D. H. Lawrence* (Bloomington: Indiana University Press, 1955), 22.

15. Ibid., 7.

16. Ibid., 100, 106, 107, 106–7.

17. Mudrick, "The Originality of *The Rainbow*," 63.

18. Ibid., 78.

19. Keith Sagar, *The Art of D. H. Lawrence* (Cambridge: Cambridge University Press, 1966), 42.

20. Ibid., 2, 3.

21. William Tiverton, *D. H. Lawrence and Human Existence* (New York: Philosophical Library, 1951), 80.

22. Goodheart, *The Utopian Vision*, 91.

23. Colin Clarke, *River of Dissolution: D. H. Lawrence and English Romanticism* (New York: Barnes & Noble, 1969), ix, 59.

24. Ibid., 46.

25. Ibid., ix.

26. Frank Kermode, *D. H. Lawrence* (New York: Viking Press, 1973), 49.

27. Scott Sanders, *D. H. Lawrence and the World of the Five Major Novels* (New York: Viking Press, 1973), 67, 68, 88, 93.

28. Marguerite Beede Howe, *The Art of the Self in D. H. Lawrence* (Athens: Ohio University Press, 1977), 1, 45.

29. Ibid., 22, 23, 28, 48.

30. Daniel Schneider, *D. H. Lawrence: The Artist as Psychologist* (Lawrence: University Press of Kansas, 1984), 1, 3, 10.

31. Ibid., 37, 39.

32. Daniel Schneider, *The Consciousness of D. H. Lawrence: An Intellectual Biography* (Lawrence, Kansas: University Press of Kansas, 1986), 16.

33. Judith Ruderman, *D. H. Lawrence and the Devouring Mother: The Search for a Patriarchal Ideal of Leadership* (Durham, N. C.: Duke University Press, 1984), 11, 17, 89, 174, 183.

Chapter 4

1. Mudrick, "The Originality of *The Rainbow*," 75.
2. *The Letters of D. H. Lawrence,* 1:403.
3. *Women in Love* (New York: Viking Compass Edition, 1960), 312.
4. *Women in Love,* 361.
5. "We Need One Another," in *Phoenix,* 190.

Chapter 5

1. Spilka, *The Love Ethic,* 95.

Chapter 6

1. Mudrick, "The Originality of *The Rainbow*," 66.
2. *Apocalypse* (New York: Viking Compass Edition, 1967), 199.

Chapter 7

1. Mudrick, "The Originality of *The Rainbow*," 74.
2. "We Need One Another," in *Phoenix,* 189.
3. *Women in Love,* 302, 311.
4. Leavis, *Novelist,* 124.
5. "We Need One Another," in *Phoenix,* 194.
6. Kinkead-Weekes, "The Marble and the Statue," 116.

Chapter 8

1. *The Letters of D. H. Lawrence,* 2:165.
2. Ibid., 2:273.

Notes

Chapter 9

1. "Morality and the Novel," in *Phoenix*, 528.
2. *The Letters of D. H. Lawrence*, 2:271–72.
3. Ibid., 2:271.

Selected Bibliography

Primary Works

The Rainbow. London: Methuen, 1915; New York: B. W. Huebsch, 1915. Published in Great Britain by Penguin Books in 1949 and as a Viking Compass Edition in the United States in 1961.

The Letters of D. H. Lawrence. 8 vols. Edited by James T. Boulton. Cambridge: Cambridge University Press, 1979–19–. When this volume went to press, five of the eight projected volumes had been published. These volumes of letters are part of the *Cambridge Edition of the Letters and Works of D. H. Lawrence.*

The Collected Letters of D. H. Lawrence. 2 vols. Edited by Harry T. Moore. New York: Viking Press, 1962. Readers will have to rely on the second volume of this fine collection of letters until the Cambridge edition is complete.

Study of Thomas Hardy. In *Phoenix: The Posthumous Papers of D. H. Lawrence,* edited by Edward D. McDonald. New York: Viking Press, 1936.

Secondary Works

Bibliographies

Cowan, James C., ed. *D. H. Lawrence: An Annotated Bibliography of Writings About Him.* Vol. 1. De Kalb: Northern Illinois University Press. Contains useful, concise annotations of works written about Lawrence and his works from 1909 through 1960.

————, ed. *D. H. Lawrence: An Annotated Bibliography of Writings About Him.* Vol. 2. De Kalb: Northern Illinois University Press, 1985. Carries on the work of vol. 1, covering the period 1961–75.

Selected Bibliography

Roberts, Warren. *A Bibliography of D. H. Lawrence*. London: Rupert Hart-Davis, 1963. The definitive bibliography of Lawrence's works.

Sagar, Keith. *The Art of D. H. Lawrence*. See listing below.

Biographies

Aldington, Richard. *D. H. Lawrence: Portrait of a Genius But . . .* London: Heinemann, 1950; New York: Duell, Sloan and Pearce, 1950. Engaging early account of Lawrence containing only scattered references to *The Rainbow*. Aldington assumes the novel is highly autobiographical.

Lawrence, Frieda. *Not I, But the Wind*. New York: Viking Press, 1934. Frieda Lawrence presents her account of a "hard" and "wonderful" relationship with Lawrence.

Moore, Harry T. *The Priest of Love: A Life of D. H. Lawrence*. Rev. ed. New York: Penguin Books, 1974. Revised, expanded, and improved version of Moore's *The Intelligent Heart: The Story of D. H. Lawrence,* originally published in 1954. A sympathetic and clear account of Lawrence's life.

Nehls, Edward, ed. *D. H. Lawrence: A Composite Biography*. 3 vols. Madison: University of Wisconsin Press, 1957–59. Piecing together portions of letters, memoirs, and other fragments of prose, Nehls produces a valuable composite of Lawrence's life. Because many points of view are included, the final assessment of Lawrence the man is left to the reader.

Literary Criticism

Ben-Ephraim, Gavriel. *The Moon's Dominion: Narrative Dichotomy and Female Dominance in Lawrence's Earlier Novels*. London and Toronto: Fairleigh Dickinson University Press, 1981. Study of Lawrence's first five novels examining the relationship of the tale to the teller. In the chapter on *The Rainbow* Ben-Ephraim stresses that the narrator does not interfere with the tale and that Lawrence explores his characters' lives from within and at the deepest level. Focusing on Ursula, he says that she progresses in stages and is ultimately fulfilled; however, her fulfillment is "inhumanly abstract" because she is not yet "balanced by a male."

Clarke, Colin. *River of Dissolution: D. H. Lawrence and English Romanticism*. New York: Barnes and Noble, 1969. In this study of Lawrence's relation to the English romantics, Clarke is most interested in *Women in Love,* but has a great deal to say about *The Rainbow*. Stressing Lawrence's discovery that there is "a virtue in degradation," he regards *The Rainbow* as a movement toward this discovery, which is articulated fully in *Women in Love*. Both books suggest that corruption, although degrading, "can also energize and renew."

Daleski, H. M. *The Forked Flame: A Study of D. H. Lawrence.* Evanston, Ill.: Northwestern University Press, 1965. Stresses Lawrence's duality, especially "the duality of male and female." Analyzing *The Rainbow*, a novel that should be read with Lawrence's *Study of Thomas Hardy* in mind, Daleski studies the first two generations of Brangwens before focusing on Ursula and her battle with Skrebensky. According to Daleski, this battle makes her realize that her "assertion" with him is a "dead end" but also that her physical being has value. Thus her vision of the rainbow at the end is "a vision of wholeness."

Draper, Ronald P. *D. H. Lawrence.* Boston: Twayne Publishers, 1964. Studies the three generations of Brangwens and concludes that the first two have only partially successful relationships. Discussing Ursula, Draper stresses that she is more complicated than her predecessors, that their problems culminate in her, and that Skrebensky is her final and greatest disillusionment. Draper comments briefly on the unsuccessful use of the rainbow and the "compelling" use of the horses at the end of the novel.

————, ed. *D. H. Lawrence: The Critical Heritage.* New York: Barnes and Noble, 1970. A collection of reviews of Lawrence's fiction, poetry, and nonfiction. Nine obituaries are also included.

Goodheart, Eugene. *The Utopian Vision of D. H. Lawrence.* Chicago: University of Chicago Press, 1963. In this provocative book Goodheart concentrates on themes instead of individual works. Presenting Lawrence as a "tablet-breaker," he discusses the novelist's response to society. Ultimately, Goodheart is most interested in the revolutionary nature of Lawrence's utopian vision. Citing *The Rainbow*, he describes that vision as "sheer oppressive emptiness" but concludes that Ursula sees a wonderful future beyond her unhappy present.

Hough, Graham. *The Dark Sun: A Study of D. H. Lawrence.* London: Gerald Duckworth and Co., 1956. Hough describes *The Rainbow* as Lawrence's attempt to present the changes that occur in the relationships of married people. Studying all three generations of Brangwens, he focuses finally on Ursula. He finds her relationship with Skrebensky confusing and her "regeneration" unconvincing. Nevertheless, he says the novel is "very fine."

Howe, Marguerite Beede. *The Art of the Self in D. H. Lawrence.* Athens: Ohio University Press, 1977. Howe concentrates on Lawrence's interest in identity and "the fragmented self." In the chapter on *The Rainbow* she draws attention to Lawrence's "new idea of personality": that individuals have a social and an essential self and, as a result, experience conflicts in their relationships. Focusing on Ursula, she emphasizes that the break with Skrebensky results from conflict but also signifies the individual's emancipation from parents, the past, and society.

Selected Bibliography

Kermode, Frank. *D. H. Lawrence.* New York: Viking Press, 1973. Kermode covers a wide range of works as he studies the relationship between Lawrence's art and his metaphysic. Commenting on *The Rainbow,* he says that "doctrine" mars the novel occasionally but that the novel succeeds ultimately because the author's metaphysic is generally part of the very "tissue of the narrative."

Kinkead-Weekes, Mark. "The Marble and the Statue." In *Twentieth Century Interpretations of "The Rainbow,"* edited by Mark Kinkead-Weekes, 96–120. Englewood Cliffs, N. J.: Prentice-Hall, 1971. Using the manuscripts and Lawrence's *Study of Thomas Hardy,* Kinkead-Weekes studies marriages and relationships in *The Rainbow.* He emphasizes that revisions made the novel increasingly less autobiographical, resulted in the transformation of Anna, and placed greater and greater emphasis on the "importance of *impersonality*" in marriage. After exploring the Will-Anna relationship in depth, Kinkead-Weekes focuses on Ursula, who fails, he says, because of her own and Skrebensky's limitations. (This essay originally appeared in *Imagined Worlds: Essays on Some English Novels and Novelists in Honour of John Butt,* ed. by Ian Gregor and Maynard Mack, 371–93, 407–10 and 412–18. London: Methuen, 1968.)

Leavis, F. R. *D. H. Lawrence: Novelist.* New York: Alfred A. Knopf, 1955. In this important study of Lawrence's tales and novels Leavis concentrates on *The Rainbow* and *Women in Love* and places their author in "the great tradition" of English literature. He does not regard *The Rainbow* as perfect because it has no real conclusion and its presentation of the Ursula-Skrebensky deadlock is drawn out. Nevertheless, he calls Lawrence a remarkable innovator and states that *The Rainbow* is "a major work by a great author."

Mudrick, Marvin. "The Originality of *The Rainbow.*" In *A D. H. Lawrence Miscellany,* edited by Harry T. Moore, 56–82. Carbondale: Southern Illinois University Press, 1959. Mudrick studies three generations of Brangwens in this "family-chronicle novel." He focuses on Lawrence's view of sex as serious and normal, on the "dying away" of the community, and on the need for individuals to find help in "a passional life." Turning to the section of the novel that deals with Ursula, he describes it as "most vexatious and unrewarding for readers," possibly because Lawrence realized his real subject was the dissolution of the community. Yet he regards the ending as positive.

Ross, Charles L. *The Composition of "The Rainbow" and "Women in Love": A History.* Charlottesville: The University of Virginia Press, 1979. In this valuable study of the many revisions of *The Rainbow* and *Women in Love* Ross studies Lawrence's evolution as a writer. At the same time, he reveals what Lawrence meant to emphasize as he progressed from "The Sisters" and "The Wedding Ring" to *The Rainbow* and *Women in Love.*

Ruderman, Judith. *D. H. Lawrence and the Devouring Mother: The Search for a*

Patriarchal Ideal of Leadership. Durham, N. C.: Duke University Press, 1984. Using psychoanalytic theory, Ruderman stresses Lawrence's misogyny, dependence on women, belief in male dominance and, especially, his ambivalence toward the devouring mother. Although she focuses on the works of the leadership period (especially *Aaron's Rod, Kangaroo,* and *The Plumed Serpent*), Ruderman also offers an excellent chapter on Lawrence's two psychology essays and insights into a variety of tales and essays. At all times, she regards Lawrence's "mother fixation" as a chief concern throughout his career.

Sagar, Keith. *The Art of D. H. Lawrence.* Cambridge: The University Press, 1966. This book about Lawrence's fiction, poetry, and nonfiction has long chapters on *The Rainbow* and *Women in Love,* and a very useful chronology of Lawrence's works. Sagar states that his aim is to "discover the 'appropriate form' which Lawrence's genius takes in all his imaginative works." In discussing *The Rainbow,* he focuses on the first two generations of Brangwens and then turns his attention to Ursula, an emancipated and uprooted female who suffers a series of disillusionments. Ultimately, he finds both Skrebensky and the rainbow symbol inadequate.

Sanders, Scott. *D. H. Lawrence: The World of the Five Novels.* New York: Viking Press, 1973. Sanders concentrates on the opposition between nature and culture in five major novels. In studying *The Rainbow* he isolates three contrasting themes: the natural self and the social self, the body and the mind, and silence and language. He believes Lawrence is dissatisfied with society and therefore sides with nature and the natural man. In keeping with this idea, Sanders maintains that Lawrence's characters "are in flight from society" beginning with the latter part of *The Rainbow.*

Schneider, Daniel J. *The Consciousness of D. H. Lawrence: An Intellectual Biography.* Lawrence: University Press of Kansas, 1986. Schneider focuses on Lawrence's sustained effort to discover a religious alternative to modern skepticism and unbelief. He cites Lawrence's sensitivity, love for others, and responsibility for others. Acknowledging that Lawrence rejected the bullying spiritual woman and Christianity's unselfish love, he says that Lawrence began to develop "his ideas about love as a religious experience" while composing *The Rainbow* and *Women in Love.*

_____. *D. H. Lawrence: The Artist as Psychologist.* Lawrence: University of Kansas Press, 1984. In this major study of Lawrence's psychology Schneider cites many parallels between Lawrence and Nietzsche, links Lawrence to Schopenhauer, stresses Lawrence's materialism, and devotes a long section to Lawrence's theory of the unconscious. Describing *The Rainbow* as "the culmination of the nineteenth-century materialism," Schneider emphasizes that the females in this book and *Women in Love* are not able to live with males who have no purpose in life beyond serving women. Nevertheless, there is one successful couple: Ursula finds the right union and balance with Rupert Birkin.

Spilka, Mark. *The Love Ethic of D. H. Lawrence.* Bloomington and London: Indiana University Press, 1955. Stressing that Lawrence was a religious writer whose goal was "organic wholeness," Spilka explores Lawrence's "love ethic," that is, Lawrence's belief that "love is a religious experience." In the chapter on *The Rainbow* he emphasizes that the first two generations of Brangwens are only partially successful in their search for a "higher form of being." Discussing Ursula, he emphasizes her rebelliousness, her relationship with Skrebensky (who is "null" at the center of his being), and her success in seeking fulfillment. Spilka believes that the "social optimism" at the end of the book "rings true."

Index

Because of the nature of this book, this index lists names, works other than *The Rainbow*, and subjects other than male-female relationships.

Index